POETICS BEFORE PLATO

POETICS BEFORE PLATO

INTERPRETATION AND AUTHORITY
IN EARLY GREEK THEORIES OF POETRY

Grace M. Ledbetter

PRINCETON UNIVERSITY PRESS   PRINCETON AND OXFORD

Copyright © 2003 by Princeton University Press
Published by Princeton University Press, 41 William Street,
Princeton, New Jersey 08540
In the United Kingdom: Princeton University Press,
3 Market Place Woodstock, Oxfordshire OX20 1SY

Library of Congress Cataloging-in-Publication Data

Ledbetter, Grace M., 1965–
　Poetics before Plato : interpretation and authority in early Greek
theories of poetry / Grace M. Ledbetter.
　　　p.　cm.
　Includes bibliographical references and index.
　ISBN 0-691-09609-0 (acid-free paper)
　1. Greek poetry—History and criticism—Theory, etc.　2. Authority
in literature.　3. Aesthetics, Ancient.　4. Poetics.　I. Title.
PA3092 .L43　2002
881′.0109—dc21　2002016913

British Library Cataloging-in-Publication Data is available

This book has been composed in Galliard

Printed on acid-free paper. ∞

www.pupress.princeton.edu

Printed in the United States of America

10　9　8　7　6　5　4　3　2　1

For Charles, Sarah, and Sophia

Contents

Acknowledgments _____

I am grateful to Swarthmore College for a Mary Alberston Faculty Fellowship in 1997–98, when I began work on this book.

In his graduate seminars on the *Iliad* and the *Odyssey*, Pietro Pucci encouraged my first work on Homer and provided the inspiring example of his distinctive fusion of close textual work with provocative theoretical and literary analysis. He has my gratitude and profound admiration.

My efforts in this project to combine literary with philosophical analysis could have had no more exacting magisterial guides than Jenny Strauss Clay and Julius Moravcsik. Each offered detailed and invaluable suggestions at several different stages. Their encouragement, generosity, and independence of mind made it possible for me to stand by my own thoughts and ideas.

Earlier versions of several chapters benefited from comments by audiences at the University of Pennsylvania, the Society for Ancient Greek Philosophy, the University of Colorado at Boulder, Swarthmore College, and Haverford College. Sarah Raff's comments led me to improve each of the first three chapters. Robert Sklenar read an earlier version of chapter 1 and gave me useful comments. David Mankin provided steadfast friendship, as always, and guided my project toward publication. John Paul Christy's skillful assistance lifted many of the burdens of completing the manuscript. I am grateful also to Chuck Myers of Princeton University Press for his humane professionalism.

In translating from the Greek, I have relied heavily on Richmond Lattimore's *Iliad* and *Odyssey*, Norman O. Brown's *Theogony*, William Race's Loeb edition of Pindar, Paul Woodruff's *Ion*, and Stanley Lombardo's and Karen Bell's *Protagoras*.

The greatest thanks belong to my husband, Charles Raff, whose tireless support, intellectual companionship, and commitment to the highest standards of thought sharpened my own thinking about Socrates and the Greek poets.

Abbreviations

CJ	*Classical Journal*
CP	*Classical Philology*
CQ	*Classical Quarterly*
DK	H. Diehls and W. Kranz, *Die Fragmente der Vorsokratiker,* 7th ed. (Berlin, 1954)
JHS	*Journal of Hellenic Studies*
QUCC	*Quaderni urbinati di cultura classica*
Rev. Etud. Grecq.	*Revue des Études Grecques*
SIFC	*Studi italiani di filologia classica*
TAPA	*Transactions and Proceedings of the American Philological Association*
WS	*Wiener Studien*

POETICS BEFORE PLATO

Introduction

Poetry, Knowledge, and Interpretation

TWO QUESTIONS, or sets of questions, motivate this study. The first concerns the views of poetry advanced in the Socratic dialogues *Apology, Ion,* and *Protagoras.* Plato's famous critique of poetry in the *Republic* looms so provocatively and so demandingly that scholars have continued to assume that the reflections on poetry in the early Socratic dialogues can only anticipate or supplement Plato's mature, systematic treatment of poetry. This assumption survives despite the wealth of current scholarship that proceeds from Vlastos's systematic division of Platonic from Socratic thought throughout a wide range of ethical, metaphysical, and epistemological issues.[1] The *Republic*'s notorious banishment of the poets relies on Plato's mature doctrines in metaphysics and psychology. Might a case be made for understanding the discussions of poetry in the *Ion* and other early dialogues as distinctively Socratic and independent of the Platonic treatment of poetry?

The second question explores the intersection of theoretical reflections on poetry in the literary and philosophical traditions. The precursors of the Platonic philosophy of poetry familiar from Book 10 of the *Republic* include contributions in Plato's earlier Socratic dialogues and in the Presocratic philosophical traditions of Heraclitus and Xenophanes. They also include, I shall suggest, the substantial theories of poetry within the poetic tradition of Homer, Hesiod, and Pindar. Commentators have recognized the existence of a theoretical dimension within this literary tradition, but the relations among the three poets' theories as well as the influence each of the three exerted on the philosophical tradition remain largely uncharted. There is no doubt that Socrates, no less than Plato, responded to the poetry of Homer, Hesiod, and Pindar. But what influence did the poets' *theories* of poetry have on Socratic thought?

---

[1] Vlastos is usually credited with initiating the now widely accepted view that the philosophy of the early Socratic dialogues is independent of Plato's mature philosophy. (See G. Vlastos, *Socrates: Ironist and Moral Philosopher* [Ithaca, 1991], pp. 45–131; T. Penner, "Socrates and the Early Dialogues," in R. Kraut, ed., *The Cambridge Companion to Plato* [Cambridge, 1992], pp. 121–169.) Contrast the arguments for a unitarian reading of the dialogues in C. Kahn, *Plato and the Socratic Dialogues: The Philosophical Use of a Literary Form* (Cambridge, 1996), and in J. Annas, *Platonic Ethics Old and New* (Ithaca and London, 1999). On some of the difficulties facing unitarian readings, see A. A. Long, "A Critical Notice of Julia Annas, *Platonic Ethics Old and New,*" *Oxford Studies in Ancient Philosophy* 19 (2000), pp. 344–349.

The answers to these two questions turn out to be connected. The Socratic dialogues, I shall argue, do indeed advance a distinctively Socratic theory of poetry, and this theory can only be accurately understood when framed as an implicit response to theories of poetry advanced within the literary tradition. Socratic poetics takes a position at arm's length from the *Republic*'s alarming conclusions that banish the poets from the state. Plato's conclusions in *Republic* Book 10 include these:

> [The poet] arouses, nourishes, and strengthens this [irrational] part of the soul and so destroys the rational one, in just the same way that someone destroys the better sort of citizens when he strengthens the vicious ones and surrenders the city to them. (605b2–5)

> Imitation . . . with a few rare exceptions, is able to corrupt even decent people, for that's surely an altogether terrible thing. (605 c5–6)

Socratic poetics, I shall show, contrasts starkly with the *Republic* by endorsing the traditional view that poetry harbors wisdom; by rejecting the view (common to Plato and to the tradition that emerges in fifth-century Athens) that credits the author with responsibility for his verses' moral content; and by claiming for the Socratic inquirer authority over the interpretation of poetry. For Plato, poetry does its audience direct and unavoidable psychological damage by fueling nonrational parts of the soul, and its status as mimesis prevents it from providing knowledge. For Socrates, by contrast, the possibility—indeed the requirement—that poetry submit to interpretation, ensures that poetry can serve its audience as a genuine source of knowledge, although not, as we shall see, the knowledge that poets traditionally purported to supply. The Socratic theory begins by engaging Homer and the Homeric theory of poetry.

Homer's, Hesiod's, and Pindar's theories of poetry should not be assimilated into a single "early Greek view of poetry,"[2] yet their variety is united, I shall suggest, by a common aim. Each of the three theories aims to minimize interpretation by poetry's audiences in an effort to maintain the poet's authority over his work. The poets' three theories nevertheless contrast strikingly, not least in their diverse methods for, and contrasting aims in, discouraging interpretation. To anticipate the Homeric theory's discouragement of interpretation, it may be helpful to consider a contemporary discussion that bears on the topic.

In her influential revisionist essay "Against Interpretation," Susan Sontag attempts to subvert the practice of interpretation, which she understands straightforwardly as the attempt to disclose meaning or content that is implicit in a work of art.[3] According to Sontag, interpretation rests on

---

[2] Contrast P. Murray, "Poetic Inspiration in Early Greece," *JHS* 101 (1981), pp. 87–100.

[3] S. Sontag, "Against Interpretation," in her *Against Interpretation and Other Essays* (New York, 1961), pp. 3–14.

misguided presuppositions; there is, in fact, no such thing as the content or meaning of a work of art. The critic's proper task is to articulate those formal elements of the work of art that shape the experience of encountering it in its sensuous immediacy. Sontag charges that practicing interpretation tends to corrupt abilities to experience the work of art truly, on a sensuous level. Her proposal would not reduce encounters with art to simple thrills or appreciative cries. She suggests, rather, that there are intricate responses to a work's form and the experience it induces in its audience. Sontag closes her essay with a dictum that has become famous: "in place of a hermeneutics we need an erotics of art."[4]

There are some striking connections between Sontag's view and Homeric poetics.[5] The approach to art Sontag prefers, the experiencing of its sensual immediacy unalloyed by interpretation, happens to coincide exactly with the core of the account of an audience's poetic experience that Homer's theory of poetry promotes. This Homeric theory identifies the "erotics" of poetry—that is, the relation that poet and audience enter into with the poem—with the sensually immediate experience of apprehending the poem. This immediacy, like the immediacy of sense experience, does not call for interpretation or evaluation that would seek to uncover the implicit meaning or content of the poem. Speaking, as Sontag does, of an erotics of art is precisely relevant, since, as we shall see, Homeric poetics literally eroticizes the audience's experience of poetry by depicting it as the erotic attraction experienced by Odysseus in his encounter with the Sirens.

Homer's theory, however, conceives of this sensually immediate poetic experience as acquiring *knowledge,* and in this important respect declines Sontag's call for an erotics of art. In describing the immediate experience of art as sensual or erotic, Sontag means to oppose it to any exertion of intellectual or rational faculties. The Homeric tradition is striking because, unlike Sontag's view, it imposes no opposition between the sensual and the intellectual experience of poetry: on the Homeric theory, the immediate, erotic experience of poetry simply *is* a kind of knowledge. This knowledge is not understanding or the derivation of general truths, but factual knowledge about the epic world. In the *Ion,* Socrates attacks the poetic tradition by denying that Homer's account of the experience of poetry is an account of knowledge. Socrates maintains instead that the experience is "inspiration," which he takes to contrast with any sort of intellectual activity and to offer, by itself, no grasp of the wisdom that poetry may have to offer.

Hesiod, we shall see, anticipates recent discussions of the unreliable narrator.[6] The radically skeptical implication of Hesiodic poetics excludes hu-

---

[4] Sontag 1961, p. 14.

[5] Sontag herself (1961, pp. 12–13) cites Auerbach's reading of Homer, which I discuss in detail in chapter 1.

[6] For a classic discussion see W. Booth, *The Rhetoric of Fiction* (Chicago, 1961), pp. 339–374.

man audiences from knowing whether the content of poetry is true. Even as Hesiod retains his Homeric precursor's opposition to hermeneutics, he produces a radically innovative poetics by inciting doubts about his poem's veracity. The aim is to frustrate the audience's efforts to interpret his verse's content, all in an effort to advance poetry's immediate, psychotherapeutic effects.

Pindar's poetics is an early expression of a central and lasting anxiety of political poetry that dreads the subversive power of unauthorized interpretations.[7] Pindar claims for the poet himself sole prerogative to interpret his poetry, which he exercises to maintain and celebrate the values of an aristocratic establishment.

Plato's dialogues *Ion* and *Protagoras* together with the *Apology* advance a Socratic poetics that would claim for poetry's audiences authority over its interpretation. Socrates' theory thus opposes the primary common theme we shall find repeated in the poets' theories. By each in their different ways discouraging interpretation, these theories promote the poet as a definitive and unquestionable authority. By the fifth century, tradition had lent its weight to a generalized version of the poets' self-promoting theories. Pindar, we shall see, explicitly claims to fill the role of moral authority. As the earliest reactions to their poems' moral content testify,[8] Homer and Hesiod too had long standing as legislators of traditional morality. The poet's role as enforcer of traditional morality was absorbed into fifth-century orthodoxy, as illustrated, for example, by the polemical opposition of Aristophanes' *Clouds* to sophistic education.[9] In Aristophanes' comedy, the sophists' intellectualist methods turn children against their parents with the idea that expert instruction, rather than the gradual process of socialization and acculturation, provides moral education.[10] The poet's success in legislating moral opinion is well illuminated in the *Apology*'s depiction of the effect of Aristophanes' *Clouds* on Socrates' reputation, and eventually on his

---

[7] For example, on the political ramifications of epic interpretation, see D. Quint, *Epic and Empire: Politics and Generic Form from Virgil to Milton* (Princeton, 1993).

[8] Xenophanes DK 22 B 11, for example, famously criticizes Homer and Hesiod for portraying the gods as engaged in morally reprehensible behavior (theft, adultery, and deception).

[9] On the poet's status as teacher in the fifth century, see B. Snell, *The Discovery of the Mind in Greek Philosophy and Literature,* trans. T. G. Rosenmeyer (New York, 1982), ch. 6 (pp. 113–135); R. Harriott, *Poetry and Criticism Before Plato* (London, 1969), pp. 105–9; J. Redfield, *Nature and Culture in the Iliad* (Chicago 1975), p. 42.

[10] See M. Nussbaum, "Aristophanes and Socrates on Learning Practical Wisdom," *Yale Classical Studies* 26 (1980), pp. 43–97. As Dover, *Aristophanes Clouds* (Oxford, 1970), p. xxiv, puts it, the charge that the tradition (ὁ δίκαιος λόγος) makes against the sophist is, in effect, that "The authority of the family and the state is undermined by rootless individuals who stimulate intellectual curiosity and independence of thought in the young and so minister to an appetite which family and state have been unable to satisfy."

life. Socrates cites the comedian and his play as responsible for dramatizing and perpetuating much of the slander behind the accusations.[11] Even the allegorical tradition, which Theagenes of Rhegium had already initiated in the late sixth century B.C. and which formally introduced a notion of interpreting the great poets, ultimately aimed to maintain, not challenge, the poets' traditional authority. In order to reconcile this traditional authority with new standards of conceptual thought, the allegorists supplied accounts of what they claimed was the poet's true meaning by proposing that abstract concepts lurked behind poetry's surface.[12] We shall see that Socrates, by contrast, undermines the poet's moral authority by challenging the poets' understanding of the meaning of their own poetry.

The Socratic discussions of poetry in the *Apology, Ion,* and *Protagoras,* I shall suggest, all center on the issue of interpretation, and variously raise the question of who is qualified to understand poetry's meaning. Socrates' guiding interest in moral knowledge leads him to this focus. The popular acknowledgment that traditional poetry is a repository of moral knowledge invites Socrates to examine those with a reputation for being able to grasp poetry's wisdom through their allegedly authoritative qualifications as interpreters. Thus, in the *Apology,* Socrates examines the poet by asking him to explain the meaning of his poetry, as in the *Ion* he examines the Homeric rhapsode's claim to know the meaning of Homeric verse. We see in the *Protagoras* that the sophists, too, had a reputation for, and a characteristic virtuosity in, interpreting poetry. In finding all of these reputed experts incompetent as interpreters of poetry, Socrates reassigns the task of interpretation to the nonexpert, and democratizes access to poetry's wisdom and moral knowledge, which Socratic theory makes available to all practitioners of the examined life.

The Socratic theory thus aims not to dispute poetry's value, but rather to challenge the idea that the poet (or rhapsode) has authoritative knowledge of this value. In the *Ion* and *Apology,* in fact, Socrates maintains the tradition that traces poetry to an inspiring divine source. But he defends a revisionary, anti-Homeric account of inspiration as a *non*cognitive state of the poet. Socrates wields his noncognitive account of inspiration against the poets' views of inspiration and against the descendent of poets' theories endorsed by traditionalism in fifth-century Athens. Socrates denies that inspiration grants knowledge and the authority knowledge carries, and maintains instead that extracting poetry's wisdom requires an act of interpretation. Interpretation reveals poetry's moral implications and exercises the same inquisitive resources that audiences apply and develop in leading

---

[11] *Apology* 18a–e.
[12] See G. Most, "The Poetics of Early Greek Philosophy," in *The Cambridge Companion to Early Greek Philosophy,* ed. A. A. Long, pp. 339–40.

an examined life. The Socratic account of inspiration thus loosens the poets' grip on poetry's moral implications and in doing so subverts the traditionalists whose views Aristophanes' comedy had dramatized.

The *Ion* and *Apology* together articulate the basic outlines of Socratic poetics. In the *Protagoras,* where Socrates interprets a poem by Simonides, Socrates further develops his view of interpretation. As we shall see, he there produces a parody of sophistical interpretation of the poem that has so far appeared merely tangential to his philosophical concerns in the dialogue. When read against the account of interpretation in Socrates' poetics, however, the passage can be seen to develop the dialogue's ongoing contrast between Socratic and sophistic methodology by offering a Socratic argument against the relativist assumptions that typically inform sophistic interpretations of poetry. In arguing against such assumptions, Socrates begins to show us what a Socratic interpretation of a poem would be.

We might note that the Socratic turn to interpretation, with its demotion of the author and its focus on the text and the act of interpretation, anticipates influential features of poststructuralist literary criticism such as Barthes's and Foucault's "death of the author" theses.[13] Yet if these current trends are understood to undermine the very concept of meaning in the text,[14] then Socrates' theory of interpretation will perhaps have more in common with New Criticism, since for him the text itself, in isolation from its author and historical factors, harbors encoded, determinate meaning. To complicate matters still further, the author in a certain way re-emerges on the Socratic view, or rather, is replaced, since Socrates holds that what gives poetry moral significance is the divine wisdom with which the gods have inspired it. The most important point to make in considering the Socratic theory of interpretation in relation to what we call literary theory, however, reveals a general point of contrast: for Socrates there is no specifically literary method to apply to the interpretation of poetry, but only the generally applicable practice of inquiry that Socrates would have humans apply to all claims to truth. Socratic interpretation turns out to be Socratic inquiry, and poetry takes its place as a source of knowledge, but not a privileged one. This leveling of poetry with other sources of human wisdom and democritization of the task of interpretation is one of the most characteristic, and most subversive, features of Socratic poetics.

Two striking conclusions emerge from examining the poets' theories of poetry and their relation to the Socratic view of poetry. The first is that the

---

[13] R. Barthes, "The Death of the Author," in *Image-Music-Text,* Essays Selected and Translated by S. Heath (New York, 1977); M. Foucault, "What is an Author?" in P. Rabinow, ed., *The Foucault Reader* (New York, 1986).

[14] A view defended by P. Lamarque, "The Death of the Author: An Analytical Autopsy," *British Journal of Aesthetics* 30 (1990), pp. 319–31.

shared aim of the poet's theories forms a tradition to which Socrates responds polemically. The second is that the distinctively Socratic poetics which results adds to the history of theories of poetry a chapter on Socratic poetics, separate from the familiar topic of Plato's treatment of poets and poetry.[15]

[15] For current interpretations of Plato's position in the *Republic* see, for example, A. Nehamas, "Plato on Imitation and Poetry in *Republic* X" and "Plato and the Mass Media," in A. Nehamas, *Virtues of Authenticity: Essays on Plato and Socrates* (Princeton, 1999), pp. 251–302; M. Burnyeat, "Culture and Society in Plato's *Republic*," in *The Tanner Lectures on Human Values* 20 (Salt Lake City, 1999), pp. 217–324.

Chapter One _____

Supernatural Knowledge in Homeric Poetics

THERE IS AN INFLUENTIAL reading of Homer that found its classic formulation in E. Auerbach's essay, "The Scar of Odysseus."[1] There, Auerbach argued that certain formal features of the *Iliad* and *Odyssey* combine to discourage any interpretation that would seek to derive from the poems implicit teachings or ulterior meaning. In Homer, Auerbach observes, all phenomena are at the fore and in focus: "never is there a form left fragmentary or half-illuminated, never a lacuna, never a gap, never a glimpse of unplumbed depths." There is never a hint that something remains to be expressed, nor a sense that events are "fraught with background." Homer articulates complexity not through implied layers of meaning, but through the succession of events and emotions, each of which presents itself, for the time it is before the audience, as a "pure present" unadorned by perspective.[2]

These successive "pure presents" that for Auerbach characterize the immediacy of Homeric narrative offer a perceptual model of poetic experience. In the Homeric poems, Auerbach says, "Delight in physical existence is everything . . . , and their highest aim is to make that delight perceptible to us."[3] This perceptual model likens reading Homer to the passive viewing of images that absorb viewers in their own reality, but prompt neither inference to generalizable truths nor to moral instruction, and so tend to suppress reflection and interpretation: "Homer can be analyzed, . . . but he cannot be interpreted."[4] Thus Auerbach famously contrasted Homeric narrative, which he claims invites no relating of our own lives, with Biblical narrative, which demands that we "fit our own life into its world, feel ourselves to be elements in its structure of universal history."[5]

C. S. Lewis offered a second and complementary account of the same peculiarity of Homeric poetry in his discussion of primary epic in *A Preface to Paradise Lost*.[6] Lewis traces the preternatural believability of Home-

---

[1] E. Auerbach, *Mimesis: The Representation of Reality in Western Literature*, trans. W. R. Trask (Princeton, 1953), pp. 1–20.

[2] P. Vivante, *The Homeric Imagination: A Study of Homer's Poetic Perception of Reality* (Bloomington and London, 1970), pp. 3–34; 120–209, echoes Auerbach's notion of a "pure present" by positing the autonomy and primacy of the "aesthetic moment" in Homeric epic.

[3] Auerbach 1953, p. 13.

[4] Auerbach 1953, p. 13.

[5] Auerbach 1953, p. 15.

[6] C. S. Lewis, *A Preface to Paradise Lost* (New York, 1961), p. 23.

ric poetry to a lack of mediation between the reader and the events of the poems. The poem's formulaic structure, based on repetition, fixes an unchanging objective background that compels the listener "to accept it as reality." Audiences experience the poem as though no poet intervened, indeed, as though no language or representation mediated their encounter with the poem. On Lewis's view, the poem itself exhibits pure experiential data of "the events themselves." "There is no use in disputing whether any episode could really have happened. We have seen it happen . . . "

Lewis cites an immediacy; Auerbach credits Homeric poetry with a kind of formal completeness and self-sufficiency. I begin by sketching this interpretation of Homer not because I find it ultimately convincing as an account of Homeric narrative—indeed many serious objections continue to be raised[7]—but because I think it owes its appeal and influence to something other than plausibility. The view fascinates in part because it confirms an experience that many of us have had reading Homer, and other great works of literature. If we agree with Harold Bloom that "one mark of originality that can win canonical status for a literary work is a strangeness that we can never altogether assimilate, or that becomes such a given that we are blinded to its idiosyncrasies,"[8] then Auerbach's and Lewis's readings of Homer confront just that exotic, near magical component that lends the poems their peculiar allure. The poems appear not to be representations at all and to win immunity from any interpretive literary criticism that would chart connections between the text and its ulterior meaning.

In this chapter I shall suggest that there is a different sort of factor at work in this classic reading of Homer, another explanation for, or interpretation of, the reading itself. Auerbach, I shall argue, read the Homeric poems not as they unambiguously are, but just as Homer wanted them to be read, that is, according to the theory of poetry the Homeric poems themselves promote—a theory designed to enchant by its alluring con-

---

[7] For example, I. J. F. De Jong, "Eurykleia and Odysseus' Scar: *Odyssey* 19.393–466," *CQ* 35 (1985), pp. 517–18, proposes that Auerbach's emblematic example, Eurykleia's recognition of Odysseus's scar at *Odyssey* 19.393–466, can be read as a flashback in Eurykleia's mind, thus contradicting Auerbach's notion that any such "subjectivistic-perspectivistic procedure, creating foreground and background" was "entirely foreign to the Homeric style" (cf. A. Köhnken, "Die Narbe des Odysseus," who argues that Homer distinguishes foreground from background by a difference in narrative style). M. Lynn-George, *Epos: Word, Narrative and the Iliad* (London, 1988), pp. 1–49, argues that the poems present indeterminate meanings and temporal movements introducing possibilities that threaten the completeness of its narrative. L. Slatkin, *The Power of Thetis* (Berkeley, 1991), pp. 114–15, shows how background and perspective are created in Homeric poetry through a process of "selection, combination, and adaptation" from mythological material known to the ancient audience. Later in this chapter I will raise some additional objections to Auerbach's theory, especially to its central claim that Homeric poetry invites no relating of our own lives.

[8] H. Bloom, *The Western Canon* (New York, 1994), p. 4.

ception of poetic experience. I shall argue that Homeric poetics, by which I mean Homer's implicit account of the connections among poem, poet, and audience, both conforms to an Auerbachean, perceptual theory of poetic experience and enlists that very theory as part of the poems' strategy for success. The Homeric theory contributes not as a disinterested account of the nature and function of Homeric poetry, but as a poetic and literary influence on the reader. Auerbach's theory, then, does not so much hold true of Homeric narrative as it does conform to the rhetoric of Homeric poetics.

It has long been established that early Greek poetry's own reflections on the nature of poetry contribute opening chapters to the history of the theory of poetry.[9] Both the *Iliad* and *Odyssey* supply Homer's self-conscious reflections about the nature of the poet and poetic discourse by representing their heroes as poet-figures: Achilles, in one of his characteristic moments, has retreated from the battlefield when he is found consoling

---

[9] On Homeric poetics alone see E. R. Curtius, *European Literature and the Latin Middle Ages* (Princeton, 1953), p. 468; W. Kraus, "Die Auffassung des Dichterberufs im früen Griechentum," *WS* 68 (1955), pp. 65–87; W. Marg, *Homer über die Dichtung* (Münster, 1971); "Das erste Lied des Demodokos," in his *Navicula Chiloniensis* (Leiden, 1956); G. Lanata, *Poetica preplatonica* (Florence, 1963); H. Maehler, *Die Auffassung des Dichterberufs im frühen Griechentum bis zur Zeit Pindars* (Göttingen, 1963); M. Treu, "Von der Weisheit der Dichter," *Gymnasium* 72 (1965), pp. 434–49; H. Koller, "ΘΕΣΠΙΣ ΑΟΙΔΟΣ," *Glotta* 43 (1965), pp. 277–85; J.-P. Vernant, *Myth et pensée chez les Grecs* (Paris, 1965), pp. 51–94; M. Detienne, *Les Maîtres de vérité dans la Grèce archaïque* (Paris, 1967); *The Masters of Truth in Archaic Greece*, trans. Janet Lloyd (New York, 1996); Harriott 1969; Douglass Stewart, *The Disguised Guest: Rank, Role, and Identity in the Odyssey* (Lewisburg, 1976), pp. 146–95; J. Svenbro, *La Parole et le Marbre* (Lund, 1976), pp. 1–73; W. Rösler, "Die Entdeckung der Fiktionalität," *Poetica* 12 (1980), pp. 283–319; Murray 1981; S. Scully, "The Bard as Custodian of Homeric Society," *QUCC* 37 (1981), pp. 67–83; C. Macleod, "Homer on Poetry and the Poetry of Homer," in his *Collected Essays* (New York, 1983); P. Murray, "Homer and the Bard," in *Aspects of the Epic*, ed. T. Winnifrith, P. Murray, and K. Gransden (London, 1983); A. Bergren, "Odyssean Temporality: Many (Re)Turns," in Rubino, C., and C. Shelmerdine, *Approaches to Homer* (Austin, 1983); W. G. Thalmann, *Conventions of Form and Thought in Early Greek Poetry* (Baltimore, 1984); B. Gentili, "Poeta e musico in Grecia," in *Oralità, Scrittura, Spettacolo,* ed. M. Vegetti (Turin. 1983); A. Thornton, *Homer's Iliad: Its Composition and the Motif of Supplication* (Göttingen, 1984), pp. 23–45; G. Walsh, *The Varieties of Enchantment: Early Greek Views of the Nature and Function of Poetry* (Chapel Hill, 1984); S. Goldhill, *The Poet's Voice: Essays on Poetics and Greek Literature* (Cambridge, 1991); D. C. Feeney, *The Gods in Epic: Poets and Critics of the Classical Tradition* (Oxford, 1991), p. 23; A. Ford, *Homer: The Poetry of the Past* (Ithaca, 1992); C. Segal, "Kleos and its Ironies in the Odyssey," in H. Bloom, ed., *Homer's Odyssey* (New York, 1988); "Bard and Audience in Homer" in *Homer's Ancient Readers,* ed. R. Lamberton and J. J. Keaney (Princeton, 1992); E. L. Bowie, "Lies, Fiction and Slander in Early Greek Poetry," in C. Gill and T. P. Wiseman, eds., *Lies and Fiction in the Ancient World* (Austin, 1993), pp. 1–37; C. Segal, *Singers, Heroes and Gods in the Odyssey* (Ithaca, 1994); L. H. Pratt, *Lying and Poetry from Homer to Pindar: Falsehood and Deception in Archaic Greek Poetics* (Ann Arbor, 1993); M. Finkelberg, *The Birth of Literary Fiction in Ancient Greece* (Oxford, 1998).

himself by playing the lyre and singing of the "fame of men," a song that could only be epic poetry; Odysseus exhibits his character through his ongoing role of storyteller, and Homer explicitly and repeatedly compares him to a bard.[10] Minor poetic personae include the bards Phemius and Demodocus, and Helen, who also contribute Homeric reflections on poetry.[11] We shall see primary exhibitions of Homer's poetic self-consciousness in the traditional invocation of the Muses, and in the figure of the Sirens. By focusing on these passages I do not claim to present an exhaustive account of Homeric reflections on poetry;[12] nor shall I propose that Homeric poetics should be understood as a theory that applies with full accuracy or without exception to Homeric poetry. I do, however, claim to uncover a poetics that the *Iliad* and *Odyssey* each employs for poetic ends.[13]

It seems reasonable to join the scholarly consensus in treating Homer himself as a protocritic, given that the *Iliad* and *Odyssey* contain elements of a theory of poetry. But unqualified, this approach can justly be accused of literary naïveté.[14] If Homer had committed his theory of poetry to writing in a philosophical treatise, like Aristotle's *Poetics*, for example, then it would be natural to grant that his treatise laid claim to represent accurately the poet's own view of his poetry. But of course the medium for Homer's theory of poetry, like Hesiod's and Pindar's, is not the philosophical treatise, but poetry itself. Homer's poetic presentation of his theory raises a set of widely neglected issues that must inform the study of Homeric poetics, and that shift some of the fundamental questions a critic must ask. Precisely

[10] On Odysseus as poet-figure, see especially J. M. Redfield, "The Making of the *Odyssey*," in A. C. Yu, ed., *Parnassus Revisited* (Chicago, 1973), p. 150; Stewart 1976; Thalmann 1984, pp. 157–84; Walsh 1984, pp. 1–21; S. Murnaghan, *Disguise and Recognition in the Odyssey* (Princeton, 1987), pp. 148–75; Goldhill 1991, pp. 1–68; Segal 1994.

[11] Menelaus and Nestor have also been seen as poet-figures. See Macleod 1983, p. 3; Thalmann 1984, p. 166.

[12] Some studies have extended the scope of inquiry by considering poetry's relation to storytelling. See, e.g., P. Mackie, "Song and Storytelling: An Odyssean Perspective," *TAPA* 127 (1997), p. 78; S. D. Olsen, *Blood and Iron: Stories and Storytelling in Homer's Odyssey* (Leiden, 1995). See also the connections drawn between poetry and supplication in K. Crotty's *The Poetics of Supplication* (Ithaca, 1994), esp. pp. 89–104, 160–210.

[13] *Pace* Finkelberg 1998, p. 29, who holds that the passages dealing explicitly with poetry "seem to support any position whatever as to the nature of traditional poetics" and that we are therefore "compelled to conclude that inductive inferences from Homer's materials on poetry to Homer's view of poetry as a whole do not constitute a satisfactory means for analysing his poetics." Finkelberg bases her conclusions on the fact that scholars have disagreed in their interpretations. Scholarly disagreement need have no such implication.

[14] The suspicion that there are likely to be extratheoretical concerns behind the poet's claims about his own poetry has been voiced by Bowie 1993, p. 12 (cf. Svenbro's (1976, pp. 29–35) proposal that behind the poet's appeals to the Muses lurk intricacies of a social dynamic between poet and audience.

because Homeric poetry's reflections on the nature of poetry are themselves ingredients of his poems, the presentation of the theory is naturally devoted to producing poetic effects. This is to say that the portions of the poems that contribute to Homer's theory are just as much poetry as any other parts. Because Homer's theory of poetry in this way functions *as poetry,* it would be erroneous to infer with any certainty that the theory straightforwardly represents Homer's understanding of poetry and of himself. For as part of the Homeric poems, the content of his theory of poetry is likely to be formulated and exploited to advance the author's literary purposes. With this caution in mind, the fundamental question the critic asks becomes not how does Homer view poetry, but rather, how does Homer *want* his poetry to be viewed, and why does he want his audience to view it that way.[15]

I shall argue that Homer wants poetry to be viewed as providing a kind of divine knowledge that has the immediacy and pleasure of sensory experience. The fact that this experience is depicted as acquiring *knowledge* has been insufficiently appreciated by commentators because of a common neglect of its crucial role in the Homeric theory and in the theory's influence.[16] According to the Homeric theory, the kind of knowledge poetry provides is quasi-perceptual knowledge of the epic world. Because the knowledge poetry offers is quasi-perceptual, it discourages interpretation that would follow its discursive path to some moral or general truth. Similarly, poetry offers its audience already complete knowledge, not material that calls for supplement by interpretation. Because the quasi-perceptual

[15] The importance of starting here, rather than with the standard question can be illustrated by an example where the historicist assumption affects the interpretation of Homer's theory. In her recent study of Homeric poetics, Finkelberg 1998, p. 68, assumes along with many others that "to the extent that he derived poetry from divine inspiration, Homer must have seen himself as a mouthpiece of the Muses." She then acknowledges a problem for this view, since it appears to conflict with a feature of the historical milieu, namely, the fact that oral poets of the Homeric age are typically credited with a considerable degree of creative freedom. How can Homer have artistic freedom and at the same time merely transmit the Muses' song? The conflict only arises if one assumes that the Homeric narrator's portrayal of the poet necessarily represents Homer's self-understanding, that the former is literally autobiographical. The assumption is easily abandoned once one acknowledges that the Homeric narrator's portrayal of the poet need not reflect Homer's understanding of himself, and instead primarily serves his literary purposes. That is to say, Homer's theory is likely to have poetic enchantment, rather than historical plausibility, as its governing concern.

[16] Critics have variously identified the Homeric conception of poetry's purpose as pleasure (E. E. Sikes, *The Greek View of Poetry* [London, 1931], pp. 1–7; A. Sperdutti, "The Divine Nature of Poetry in Antiquity," *TAPA* 81 (1950), p. 227; Ford 1992, p. 49–51; 83–84), as forgetfulness of self and present circumstances (Walsh 1984, p. 14), as "vividness" (Ford 1992, pp. 49–56), or as knowledge of a different kind than what I describe here (moral instruction: W. Jaeger, *Paideia,* vol. 1, trans. G. Highet [Oxford, 1947], p. 36; Sperdutti 1950, pp. 227–29; understanding: Kraus 1955, p. 71; Macleod 1983, pp. 6–8; Thalmann 1984, p. 183; Crotty 1994, p. 183).

knowledge that poetry offers belongs fundamentally among the privileges of divinity, this quasi-perceptual knowledge is, according to the Homeric theory, divine knowledge.

Homer wants poetry to be viewed just this way not because he aims for a theoretically satisfactory conception of his poetry, but mainly because his theory serves his poetic purposes in two basic ways. First, the theory's account of poetic enchantment itself contributes to the audience's enchantment by promoting its alluring conception of poetic experience; viewing Homeric poetry in accordance with the theory it depicts is itself intended to enchant.[17] The theory serves this poetic aim despite its partial inaccuracy as a general description applicable to all of Homer's poetry. As we shall see, passages of Homeric poetry invite just the sort of interpretation that Homer's theory would discourage. For example, just those passages that depict poets, poetry, and audiences as subject matter—the Sirens, the invocations, and the bards' performances—all call on the audience for a modicum of theoretical reflection and identification with the poems' depicted audiences. These, in fact, belong among the most alluring passages in Homer *precisely because* they invite the reader to relate himself to part of the poem's action, or to reflect critically on his own nature as an audience. So the very passages that themselves articulate and promote Homer's theory of poetry violate the theory's antitheoretical promptings and contradict its implication that poetry discourages the reader from relating himself and his own life to the poem. And they do so, I suggest, with no consequent loss of poetic effect. If Homer's theory of Homeric poetry is inaccurate as a general account of Homeric narrative, it follows that Homer's poetry is limited theoretically. But in practical terms this limitation is beside the point, since, as I will suggest, the final question about the Homeric theory of poetry asks not whether it accurately describes the poems, but whether it advances its poetic ends. I shall argue that it can accomplish its aim of enchanting, despite its theoretical shortcomings.

A second way that the theory serves Homer's rhetorical purposes might be said to promote a *political* aim. By discouraging interpretation, the theory tends to preserve the poet's exclusive authority by exempting his poetry from interpretation and by immunizing it against evaluation. We shall see that Hesiod and Pindar maintain this political aim, thereby establishing a theoretical tradition which later attracted Socrates' scrutiny.

---

[17] This connection between poetry and the supernatural is not, then, just a historical given (Sikes 1931, p. 3; Ford 1992; Vernant 1965; Detienne 1967), but a conception posited and exploited by Homer for poetic effect as part of the poems' rhetorical strategies, a conception crafted to seduce the audience, and contribute its part in poetic experience. My interest is less in the historical question of poetry's links with magic and the supernatural than in the rhetorical uses Homeric poetry makes of these links.

Poetry and Knowledge

Let us first consider the Homeric conception of poetry's effect on its listener, paying particular attention to the poetic effects for which this conception strives. It should already be clear that I am not here interested in the historical task of reconstructing an account of the ancient audience's experience of poetry.[18] The ancient audience's experience concerns me less than the question of how the poet's or the tradition's representation of the audience's experience contribute to the poem's artistic project. It is a separate question, and one which I address in this chapter, to what extent the poems can succeed in achieving the poetic effects for which they strive. This is not an historical question, but, as we shall see, a matter of whether the Homeric theory's shortcomings as an account of Homeric narrative necessarily interfere with the theory's intended poetic effects.

There can be little doubt that the Homeric poems present poetry as a source of pleasure; this point has met with little or no controversy among the critics.[19] We are told, for example, that the bard Demodocus's gift is his power to please through song. When poetry arouses pain or grief, as in the case when Odysseus weeps in reaction to hearing tales of Troy, it disappoints traditional expectations.[20] The association of poetry with pleasure recurs throughout the *Odyssey*[21]; in the *Iliad* it appears as Achilles' "delighting his heart in the lyre" as he sings epic poetry.[22]

Both the *Iliad* and *Odyssey* also represent poetry as imparting knowledge. The extent to which the *Iliad* and *Odyssey* associate poetry with conveying knowledge has not always been fully appreciated; similarly unappreciated has been the nature of that knowledge and of its object. Those who have credited knowledge with a role in Homeric poetics have presupposed that "knowledge" is confined to moral lessons or to general truths, so they cannot avoid the objection pressed by A. Ford, who observes that acquiring knowledge from poetry by a process of interpretation or inference must unavoidably break the spell of the immediate and transporting sensory pleasure that poetry claims to offer its listener.[23] I will suggest that

[18] Others have done so. See especially Slatkin 1991; Feeney 1991; and Segal 1992. See also the cautions in G. Nagy, "Early Greek Views of Poets and Poetry," in *The Cambridge History of Literary Criticism. Vol. I: Classical Criticism* (Cambridge, 1989), p. 1.

[19] Although some (e. g., Jaeger 1947, Kraus 1955, Macleod 1983, Thalmann 1984, Crotty 1994) have focused more on poetry's intent to instruct or bring about understanding.

[20] So too when the bard's song triggers Penelope's memory of Odysseus at *Odyssey* 1. 328–44, a passage I discuss in detail below.

[21] *Odyssey* 8. 44–45; cf. also *Odyssey* 17. 385; 17. 519; 1. 347.

[22] *Iliad* 9. 186–89.

[23] Ford 1992, p. 52.

those who have seen that knowledge plays a central role in Homer's poetics apply a conception of what Homer may count as knowledge that is too narrow to include the singular conception of knowledge and of poetic experience that distinguishes the Homeric view of poetry.

In Book 8 of the *Odyssey*, after he has already heard the bard sing two songs, Odysseus tests Demodocus to discover whether he truly possesses the "magical gift of singing."[24] The fact that Odysseus assays the talent of Demodocus is interesting in itself, as it plays on the themes of test and trial that dominate Book 8 where Odysseus finds himself subject to the undercurrent of suspicion beneath the Phaeacians' hospitality.[25] The nature of the test Odysseus imposes on Demodocus speaks directly to our topic, as it discloses an account of poetry's purpose. Odysseus promises that, on condition that Demodocus's song presents an accurate recounting of the Trojan horse episode, he will spread his fame as a singer: "If you can tell me the course of these things as they happened (*kata moiran*), I will speak of you before all mankind, and tell them how freely the goddess gave you the magical gift of singing."[26] Although the meaning of the phrase *kata moiran* may extend beyond factual accuracy to include both social propriety and scrupulousness of detail,[27] it nevertheless includes within those notions the idea of factual accuracy. In this particular context, questions of accuracy and fullness of detail are paramount: because of his historical relation to the events involving the Trojan horse, Odysseus possesses precisely the expertise to evaluate the accuracy and completeness of Demodocus's account. Odysseus's reaction testifies that Demodocus sings as if he had been there himself (491): Odysseus weeps uncontrollably, and Alcinoos must stop the bard's performance. Odysseus's test presumes that good poetry conveys knowledge; not any knowledge of general truths or moral lessons, but of a full account and accurate report of the particular facts elaborated as if by a witness's testimony.[28]

In a scene we will discuss in further detail below, the poet uses the figure of the Sirens to display some general features of poetry's allure. The

---

[24] *Odyssey* 8. 485–538.

[25] See G. Rose, "The Unfriendly Phaeacians," *TAPA* 100 (1969), pp. 387–406.

[26] *Odyssey* 8. 496.

[27] On the meaning of the phrase *kata moiran*, see T. B. L. Webster, "Greek Theories of Art and Literature Down to 400 B.C.," *CQ* 33 (1939), p. 175; Svenbro 1976, pp. 24–26; A. T. Cole, "Archaic Truth," *QUCC*, n. s. 13 (1983), p. 14; Walsh 1984, pp. 16–17; Ford 1992, pp. 122–23.

[28] In this passage Homer thus suggests that poetry does not have the status of dogma: Odysseus's testing of Demodocus presumes that poetry can be either right or wrong and that accepting it as true is not simply a matter of the poet's religious or social authority (contrast Detienne 1996, p. 52). Homer's audience lacks Odysseus's unique vantage point from which to evaluate poetry's truth-value, but poetry's truth is nevertheless a matter of accuracy, not sheer authority.

Sirens, whose role in many ways matches the Muses', promise that their song will give Odysseus both pleasure *and* knowledge: when a man has heard the Sirens, "he goes away pleased and knowing more."[29] The type of knowledge they claim to impart is at once factual and complete. Command of such knowledge is the special privilege of divinity: "For we know all the toils that in wide Troy the Argives and Trojans endured through the will of the gods, and we know all the things that come to pass upon the fruitful earth."[30]

The *Iliad*'s narrator indirectly reveals that he shares the same presumption about poetry, as he intimates that his knowledge is more than merely human. In the invocation preceding the catalogue of ships in Book 2 of the *Iliad,* the poet emphasizes the Muses' direct vision of their epic subject matter:

Ἔσπετε νῦν μοι, Μοῦσαι Ὀλύμπια δώματ᾽ ἔχουσαι—
ὑμεῖς γὰρ θεαί ἐστε, πάρεστέ τε, ἴστέ τε πάντα,
ἡμεῖς δὲ κλέος οἶον ἀκούομεν οὐδέ τι ἴδμεν—
οἵ τινες ἡγεμόνες Δαναῶν καὶ κοίρανοι ἦσαν·

Tell me now, Muses that have dwellings on Olympos—
For you are goddesses, and are present, and know all things,
Whereas we hear mere rumor and know not anything—
Who were the captains of the Danaans and their lords?

(2. 484–87)

Here the poet appears to include himself in the "we" of mortals who lack the Muses' knowledge. But are we to understand that he invokes the Muses' divine knowledge only to make it clear that, like his audience, he will repeat mere hearsay in the forthcoming catalogue? Surely such a deflationary message has no place here, as the invocation builds anticipation and promises its audience something extraordinary. What then, does the poet intend by delimiting so firmly the Muses' knowledge from mere mortal hearsay? The distinction, I suggest, positions the poet to promise his audience access to something superior to mere rumor—perhaps access to divine knowledge. The poet's self-deprecatory rhetoric draws attention to the limitations of human apprehension with an aim not to reinforce or to maintain those limits, but on the contrary to suggest that his audience can transcend them through the medium of his poetry. The poet implies that because of his connection to the Muses—and we shall consider the nature of that connection—his poetry offers an extraordinary access to divine

---

[29] *Odyssey* 12. 188: ἀλλ᾽ ὅ γε τερψάμενος νεῖται καὶ πλείονα εἰδώς.

[30] *Odyssey* 12. 188–91. Alcinoos's remarks to Odysseus at *Odyssey* 11. 362–69 also assume that poets speaks "knowledgeably" (ἐπισταμένως, 368). Walsh finds here a suggestion that receiving this knowledge does not require interpretation.

knowledge, wholly distinct from routine human hearsay. He boasts not straightforwardly like a Siren, but indirectly, of his role as vehicle: the Muses convey knowledge to the audience through him.[31]

It follows that the poet contributes very differently from any ordinary mortal who gathers information by hearsay. The poet characterizes his liminal status with this suggestion that he gains the knowledge he conveys by superhuman means. He does not claim, but neither does he disavow, that his relation to the Muses elevates him to the Muses' first-person privilege of witnessing epic events, but he does imply that he reports more than mere hearsay. What exactly is the nature of the poet's relation to the Muses? The poet leaves it unresolved, and open to curiosity. One alternative conspicuously left open would credit the poet with knowledge that is not in any way inferior to a witness's firsthand perceptual knowledge. But this passage only hints at such a possibility by suggesting that the poet's relation to the Muses is something special among humans. This deliberate mystification of the relation between poet and Muse, belongs, I suggest, to Homer's rhetoric of enchantment. It prompts curiosity and seduces his audience by omitting explicitly to disclose just what lies at the source of poetry's allure. Clarity and precise distinctions may not be as seductive as Homer's *suggestion* that the poet's relation to his source engages some means of transmission other than the mundane channels for receiving human knowledge.

The poet's liminal status is alluded to further by the special connection to the divine claimed by Phemius, displayed by Demodocus,[32] and depicted still more forcefully by Helen's and by Achilles' roles as poet-figures. Achilles fills a poet's role not at all figuratively, and more literally than Odysseus does, since we find Achilles actually singing epic poetry with a lyre in the scene when the embassy approaches.[33] The poet emphasizes the pleasure Achilles receives from his own singing:

τὸν δ' εὗρον φρένα τερπόμενον φόρμιγγι λιγείῃ,
καλῇ δαιδαλέῃ ἐπὶ δ' ἀργύρεον ζυγὸν ἦεν,
τὴν ἄρετ' ἐξ ἐνάρων πόλιν Ἠετίωνος ὀλέσσας·
τῇ ὅ γε θυμὸν ἔτερπεν, ἄειδε δ' ἄρα κλέα ἀνδρῶν.

and they found Achilles delighting his heart in a lyre, clear-sounding, splendid and carefully wrought, with a bridge of silver upon it,

---

[31] Contrast Ford 1992, p. 86, who claims that the poet promises his audience only *kleos*, "an inevitable reduction from divine knowledge." The poet may say that *kleos* is all that mortals usually have access to, but he implies that his poetry gives them access to much more.

[32] Phemius invokes his connection with Apollo as grounds for Odysseus' sparing his life (*Odyssey* 22. 344–349). Demodocus is described as god-inspired (e.g., *Odyssey* 8. 43–44; 63–65), as Odysseus' test of him is taken to prove (cf. *Odyssey* 8. 487–498).

[33] On Achilles as poet see B. Hainsworth ed., *The Iliad: A Commentary Volume III: books 9–12*, Cambridge, 1993 pp. 37, 88; F. Frontisi-Ducroux, *La cithare d'Achille*, Rome, 1986.

which he won out of the spoils when he ruined Eëtion's city.
With this he was delighting his heart, and singing of men's fame.

(*Iliad* 9. 186–89)

This scene has typically been read as a reflection of poetry's association with withdrawal from action and social intercourse,[34] but it also specifically evokes the poet's privileged connection to the divine. Achilles, having withdrawn to the shore from the battle and society, sits on the border where the mortal and immortal meet, since for him the sea serves as emblem of his goddess mother. Helen, too, sits sequestered from society in her bedroom weaving intricate representations of the war into cloth. This metaphorical poetry making links her with the divine because of her great distance from, and meticulous observation of, mortal society, and because of the immortal *kleos* that we know poetry grants her.[35]

So far, then, we have seen Homeric poetics claim that poetry imparts knowledge to its audience. This knowledge consists in precise and exhaustive factual knowledge of selected episodes from the Trojan war and the events surrounding it. The Muses are depicted as witnessing the events firsthand, that is, as having perceptual knowledge of them. We have also seen the beginnings of a rhetorical pattern of suggestion and ambiguity in which the *possibility* emerges that the poet, through his special association with the divine, may come to know these facts in the privileged way the Muse does, that is, as a first-person witness.

The Object of Knowledge

Poetry imparts factual knowledge, but the precise nature of that knowledge will depend on the categorical nature of its object. Are these facts presented as belonging to an historical, although distant, past, or as somehow ahistorical and outside of the temporal realm? Or are they presented as fictional? Are the Muses thought of as repositories of history, as personifications of cultural memory, as media for access to and knowledge of a real, ahistorical realm, or as sources of a narrative tradition?[36]

We should again resist historicizing assumptions that would reduce these questions to inquiries into the "archaic mindset." The metaphysics of Homeric poetics may or may not be the conventional product of a particular,

[34] See Thalmann 1984, p. 176; Murhnaghan 1987, p. 151; Segal 1992, pp. 13, 22.

[35] See N. Austin, *Helen of Troy and Her Shameless Phantom*, (Ithaca 1994) pp. 28–29, on Helen and Achilles in this regard.

[36] Commentators have explored many of these possibilities. See, for example, A. Setti, "La memoria e il canto: Saggio di poetica arcaica greca," *SIFC* 30 (1958), pp. 129–71; Macleod 1983, pp. 5–6; Segal 1992, p. 28; Detienne 1996, pp. 149–50, n. 1.

primitive mentality. Homer's theory, however, undeniably belongs among the devices that the poet, or the tradition, employs with a certain self-consciousness, as part of its rhetoric of enchantment. This tradition will of course be shaped and limited by its particular historical mindset, but that fact does not prevent the theory from serving some *literary* function. It seems reasonable to expect, then, that the Homeric theory's metaphysics of poetry's object will itself aim to enchant the audience as part of the story that Homeric poetics tells about poetry.

Because the theory aims to enchant, it cannot self-consciously embrace the notion that the Muses convey literary fiction as such. One can agree that a nascent conception of literary fiction may underlie the *Odyssey*'s recognition that not all singers tell the truth.[37] It is an entirely different question, however, whether Homeric poetics views the *genuinely inspired* poet as relating fiction and thus *promotes* a conception of poetry as fiction. Again, our question asks how Homer wants his poetry to be viewed. Homer, I would suggest, does not want us to view poetry's subject matter as fictional because viewing it as such would undermine the more alluring possibility that poetry reports something remote, but *real*. Both the *Iliad* and the *Odyssey* in fact depict poetry's subject matter as real, at the same time they deliberately obscure its precise temporal status. An odd tension regarding temporality surfaces, for example, in the Sirens' speech to Odysseus. We have seen that the Sirens boast directly of poetry's power. Here they defend their ability to impart knowledge:

> ἴδμεν γάρ τοι πάνθ᾽ ὅσ᾽ ἐνὶ Τροίῃ εὐρείῃ
> Ἀργεῖοι Τρῶές τε θεῶν ἰότητι μόγησαν
> ἴδμεν δ᾽ ὅσσα γένηται ἐπὶ χθονὶ πουλυβοτείρῃ.

> For we know all the toils that in wide Troy
> the Argives and Trojans endured through the will of the gods,
> and we know all things that come to pass upon the fruitful earth.
>
> (12. 189–91)

The Sirens first describe their song's subject matter as events of the past— what the Trojans and Argives endured. But they immediately complicate

---

[37] Odysseus, for example, is a poet figure who often deceives his audience. In addition, as Bowie 1993, p. 16, rightly points out, Odysseus's test of Demodocus's knowledge in *Odyssey* 8 "shows that the poet can conceive of a singer who sings something that has not 'actually' happened." I would argue, however, that, on the Homeric view, such fictional songs do not proceed from a truly inspired poet. Later in this chapter I will suggest that because Odysseus lacks the genuine poet's particular connection to the Muses, he cannot contribute to the Homeric representation of the true (i.e., inspired) poet. Furthermore, it does not seem to me reasonable to infer, as Bowie does, that Phemius's song in *Odyssey* 1 contains the falsehood that Odysseus has perished; Penelope's reaction would be justified by her naturally associating him with those who had indeed perished, together with her uncertainty regarding her husband's fate.

that straightforward temporal frame by allowing, although not requiring, the reader to take the "things that come to pass upon the fruitful earth" as a separate category.[38] Through the parallel placement of ἐνὶ Τροίῃ εὐρείῃ and ἐπὶ χθονὶ πουλυβοτείρῃ, the poet can be taken to distinguish the two realms: the Sirens know *both* the events of the Trojan war *and* all things that come to pass upon the earth. This evidently categorical separation intimates that the events the Sirens portray in their song did not come to pass on the earth. The precise status of such events is not directly specified. But the suggestion that they do not occur on earth would locate them outside the human temporal framework. This suggestion's ambiguity has a rhetorical force that, appropriately enough for a Sirens' song, enchants the audience with the otherworldly mystery of poetry's subject matter.

In the *Iliad* we find a similar temporal ambiguity. In the invocation to the catalogue of ships, we have seen that the poet indirectly promises the audience something more than mere rumor. He does so by invoking the Muses' epistemological privilege:

Ἔσπετε νῦν μοι, Μοῦσαι Ὀλύμπια δώματ᾽ ἔχουσαι—
ὑμεῖς γὰρ θεαί ἐστε, πάρεστέ τε, ἴστέ τε πάντα,
ἡμεῖς δὲ κλέος οἶον ἀκούομεν οὐδέ τι ἴδμεν—
οἵ τινες ἡγεμόνες Δαναῶν καὶ κοίρανοι ἦσαν·

Tell me now, Muses that have dwellings on Olympos—
For you are goddesses, and are present, and know all things,
Whereas we hear mere rumor and know not anything—
Who were the captains of the Danaans and their lords?

(2. 484–87)

The Muses know who the captains of the Danaans and their lords were because they are present and know all things. The paradox of this formulation lies in the shift of tenses, for why should the Muses' presence (presence where?) explain their knowledge of the past? The suggestion may be that the Muses have the peculiar ability to experience the past directly. In this case, the events that make up poetry's subject matter would form part of human history. The Muse's knowledge, however, could be considered "memory" only in an extended sense that includes knowing a past object in a way that present objects are known. Here conflating Homer's portrait of the Muses with Hesiod's would mislead, since, where Hesiod connects the Muses essentially with memory, Homer specifies this quasi-perceptual knowledge of a past object as their characteristic faculty.[39]

Alternatively, the passage can be read to suggest that the Muses report

---

[38] Alternatively, one can understand the events of the Trojan war as one subset of all the things that come to pass on the earth. Since both readings are possible, the ambiguity stands.

[39] See *Theogony* 53–54.

events that exist in an eternal present, outside of the human temporal framework.[40] On this reading, poetry's subject matter would not form part of human history, but would rather be part of a legendary (but not *fictional*) realm. On both readings poetry's subject matter is real, and the Muses' divine knowledge differs from human knowledge in kind, not just in degree.[41] If the Muses have direct perceptual knowledge of the past, then they have access to the past in a way that ordinary human faculties do not. If they have direct perceptual knowledge of an ahistorical, legendary realm, then not only the *way* they know exercises a superhuman faculty of apprehension, but the object of their knowledge differs in kind from those to which humans ordinarily have access. Our passages stop short of clarifying their provocative metaphysics, and they do so deliberately, in order to magnify poetry's allure. Little ambiguity remains, however, concerning the claim that the Muses' divine knowledge differs in kind from ordinary human knowledge in its direct, perceptual apprehension of epic events.

The Poet

The Muses, then, are presented as having divine knowledge that differs in kind from human knowledge. But how does the *poet* gain access to this knowledge, and how is he able to convey it? Commentators have disagreed on whether the poet is or is not depicted as a prophet with direct vision of the events he relates. In my view the disagreement misses the point. Instead of providing clear evidence in favor of a single view of the poet, Homer repeatedly exploits the problem and the ambiguity of the poet's status, and—quite deliberately—excites speculation. The controversy in the secondary literature with regard to these questions rests in part on overly simple methods of reading the crucial passages. Murray, for example, appeals to the invocation of the catalogue of ships and to *Odyssey* 8. 489–91 to dispute Detienne's view that the poet is a prophet with direct vision of the events he relates.[42] On her view, these passages show that the poet does not have a direct, prophetic vision, but rather, "communicates" with the Muses. Murray suggests that this "communication" serves, perhaps, as a metaphor for poetic imagination. But to contend either that these passages endorse the prophetic view or the nonprophetic view of the poet is to misread their rhetorical mode. For instead of providing clear evidence

---

[40] See Vernant 1965, pp. 75–80; W. Schadewalt, *Von Homers Welt und Werk* (Stuttgart, 1965), p. 82; M. Puelma, "Der Dichter und die Wahrheit in der griechischen Poetik von Homer bis Aristoteles," *Museum Helveticum* 46 (1989), pp. 121–32, with further bibliography on the poet's "presence" at the event.

[41] *Pace* Snell 1982, p. 137; cf. Finkelberg 1998, pp. 97–98.

[42] Murray 1981, p. 93.

in favor of a single view of the poet and his gift, both passages primarily exploit the problem and the ambiguity of the poet's status, and raise the question of *possible* answers.

The invocation to the catalogue of ships indeed omits any explicit portrayal of the poet as endowed with direct vision of the events that he relates; the Muses "tell" the poet what he wants to know, and they "call the events to his mind" (μνησαίαθ', 2. 492). From the Muses' telling, as I have argued, the poet implies that he commands access to information much higher in quality than mere rumor, to nothing less than supernatural knowledge. This implication introduces problems left unanswered: how can the poet, a mere mortal, command superhuman knowledge? *Can* a human convey knowledge that is superhuman? Mortals, we have just been told, hear rumor only. The suggestion is that the poet transcends mortal limitations. The language of communication must not be presumed to hold literally, for the Muses' "telling" the poet, and "calling facts to his mind" could easily stand metaphorically for a state of prophetic vision, or for some other state in which the poet acquires supernatural knowledge. But our passage does not go that far. At the questions of the poet's superhuman resources and his liminal status, it stops short. Once again, the poet incites speculation by hedged intimations, even more effective, moving, and appropriate than would be any explicit boast of superhuman power.

A similarly indeterminate vision emerges from Odysseus's remarks to Demodocus at *Odyssey* 8. 489–91:

λίην γὰρ κατὰ κόσμον Ἀχαιῶν οἶτον ἀείδεις,
ὅσσ' ἔρξαν τ' ἔπαθόν τε καὶ ὅσσ' ἐμόγησαν Ἀχαιοί,
ὥς τέ που ἢ αὐτὸς παρεὼν ἢ ἄλλου ἀκούσας.

For well and truly do you sing of the fate of the Achaeans,
all they did and suffered and the toils they endured,
as though you yourself were there or heard it from another.

Here too, the poem provocatively incites speculation about the source of the poet's remarkable abilities. According to Murray, the passage shows that the poet lacks any direct, prophetic vision. In her view, the possibility that Odysseus mentions, of Demodocus's having heard of the sufferings of the Achaeans from someone else, remains "somewhat difficult to reconcile with the notion that he was given a personal vision of them."[43] Murray correctly notes that what amazes Odysseus is the vividness of Demodocus's account, but she misses entirely the force of line 491. Odysseus compliments the bard and expresses his amazement in a counterfactual: it is *as though* the bard were there himself *or* heard it from another (who presumably had been there himself). Only a hasty reading would take the alter-

[43] Murray 1981, p. 93.

natives Odysseus formulates to exhaust the real possibilities. Odysseus's remarks, rather, leave us in amazement over the bard's powers of vivid representation, and wondering about the source of those powers. How is it that the bard appears as though he himself had been there or had heard it from someone else who was there? One possibility is that the bard heard of the events from the Muses, who, as we have seen, are present at the scene of epic events. Another possibility, compatible with, and perhaps even advanced by Odysseus's remarks, supposes, as Vernant and Detienne suggest, that the bard himself enjoys a direct vision of epic events.[44] But rather than pointing determinately at one particular view of the source of the poet's powers, this passage, like the previous passage, prompts us to credit the poet with mysterious, uncanny, and divine power. A divine power is implied by the problem that emerges: how can a mortal poet speak as only a divinity can, as though he were present at the events themselves or heard a report from someone who was present? Both alternatives, witnessing a supernatural event and hearing about one from a witness, are inaccessible to mortals, but within the ken of the Muses. By praising Demodocus as he does, then, Odysseus compares the poet to the divine Muses themselves.

So far the notion that the poet shares the Muses' divine knowledge has emerged only through patterns of suggestion and ambiguity. When we turn to the conventional structure of invocation throughout the *Iliad* and *Odyssey,* however, this suggestion becomes a concrete formulation. In the beginning of both poems, before the catalogue of ships, and in other instances of invocation and pseudoinvocation, the poet portrays the poem's narrative voice *both* as his own, and as the Muse's. In this topos of invocation, the poet's and the Muse's voices merge:

Μῆνιν ἄειδε, θεά, Πηληϊάδεω Ἀχιλῆος
οὐλομένην, ἣ μυρί᾽ Ἀχαιοῖς ἄλγε᾽ ἔθηκε,
πολλὰς δ᾽ ἰφθίμους ψυχὰς Ἄϊδι προΐαψεν
ἡρώων, αὐτοὺς δὲ ἑλώρια τεῦχε κύνεσσιν
οἰωνοῖσί τε πᾶσι, Διὸς δ᾽ ἐτελείετο βουλή,
ἐξ οὗ δὴ τὰ πρῶτα διαστήτην ἐρίσαντε
Ἀτρεΐδης τε ἄναξ ἀνδρῶν καὶ δῖος Ἀχιλλεύς.
    Τίς τ᾽ ἄρ σφωε θεῶν ἔριδι ξυνέηκε μάχεσθαι;
Λητοῦς καὶ Διὸς υἱός·

Sing, goddess, the anger of Peleus' son Achilles
and its devastation, which put pains thousandfold upon the Achaians,
hurled in their multitudes to the house of Hades strong souls

---

[44] Demodocus's blindness of course prevents his direct vision from exercising any human faculty of vision. The Muses' perceptual knowledge too, cannot employ an ordinary human faculty of sense perception since, as we have seen, their divine perceptual knowledge differs in kind from human perceptual knowledge.

of heroes, but gave their bodies to be the delicate feasting
of dogs, of all birds, and the will of Zeus was accomplished
since that time when first there stood in division of conflict
Atreus' son the lord of men and brilliant Achilleus.
What god was it then set them together in bitter collision?
Zeus' son and Leto's, Apollo . . .

(Iliad 1. 1–9)

The dialogic structure of the poet's request in line 1 presupposes that his narrative voice is distinct from the Muses'; he asks her to sing. Yet the Muses' "reply," beginning in line 9, merges the two voices by standing formally both as the direct discourse of the goddess's response, and as the poet's narrative voice. Lines 8 and 9 in particular deliberately thwart efforts to identify the voice that will proceed to narrate. Is the "reply" spoken by the poet or by the Muse? The same pattern of ambiguity emerges in the invocation at the beginning of the *Odyssey* (10–13): "From some point, goddess, daughter of Zeus, speak and begin our story / Then all the others, as many as fled sheer destruction, / were at home, having escaped the sea and the fighting. / This one alone, longing for his wife and homecoming . . . " When the story proper begins, it is unclear whether the poet or the Muse is speaking. Other invocations and pseudoinvocations, throughout the *Iliad* especially, show the same structure.[45] The ambiguity of voice generates a view of the poet as possessed by the Muse, although not necessarily "ecstatically" possessed. By declining to distinguish the poet's from the Muse's voice, the poem promotes the poet as the voice of the divine, and it presents the poem as a direct link to the events at Troy. The Muse speaks "through" the poet in such a way that their voices are indistinguishable into human and divine elements.[46] We can say, then, that the poet transmits poetry "supernaturally" because his song transmits the Muse's divine voice. Poetry in this way presents itself as the audience's connection to the supernatural.

It has been often rightly observed that Homer nowhere depicts a poet in the state of ecstasy that elsewhere marks those who are divinely possessed.[47] Nevertheless, supernatural possession is implied in the fusion with the Muse necessary for the poet's transmission of poetry. The poems, I have argued, do allude to supernatural possession; poet and Muse merge in the transmission of poetry. Possession and ecstasy are linked in the contexts of

---

[45] Cf. *Odyssey* 1. 1ff.; *Iliad* 2. 761ff.; 11. 218ff; 14. 508ff.; 16. 112ff.; 5. 703ff.; 8. 273ff.; 11. 299ff.; 16. 692ff.

[46] Others have claimed that the Muse is herself the narrator of the poem, but this overlooks the other side of the conflated Muse-poet pair. See Clay 1983, p. 34; Murnaghan 1987, p. 171; R. J. Rabel, *Plot and Point of View in the Iliad* (Ann Arbor, 1997), pp. 33–43.

[47] See E. R. Dodds, *The Greeks and the Irrational* (Berkeley, 1951), p. 82, who assumes that possession entails ecstasy.

oracles and prophetic divination, but not in Homer's theory of the poet, since unlike the Pythia's ecstatic connection to Apollo, the poet connects to the divine cognitively. The poet collects what the Muse conveys to him by knowing it; his role as medium does not require that he become "out of his mind" in ecstasy. It does require that he share with the Muses and convey to a human audience cognition that remains divine.[48] The poet's cognitive connection to his superhuman resource implies that the Muse shares with him the knowledge she has as her firsthand vision of her subject matter.

The Audience

We have seen, then, that the *Iliad* and *Odyssey* convey a view on which poetry imparts factual knowledge to its audience. Such knowledge is conveyed through the medium of the poet, whose direct link with divinity informs his art. The pieces are now in place to draw certain conclusions about the nature of the audience's experience of poetry. Recall, first of all, the Homeric view of poetic knowledge. In the invocation to the catalogue of ships, the categorical distinction between mortals, who hear rumor only, and the goddesses, who have knowledge, makes it clear that knowing is the privilege of gods, and that there is therefore no knowledge of poetry's subject matter without a supernatural connection. But, as the Sirens' words in the *Odyssey* suggest, the audience is said to gain new knowledge from poetry. If the audience receives poetic knowledge, and there is no knowledge of poetry's subject matter absent a supernatural connection, then the audience too, the poet suggests, must become connected to the supernatural. The connection is joined by the poet, but it supplies knowledge undiminished, provided that the poet relays the divine knowledge he secures through his supernatural connection to the Muse. Homer thus allows us to view poetry as the medium through which an audience may obtain the same direct perceptual experience of epic events that the Muse and inspired poet enjoy.

As we shall see shortly, the Sirens episode in the *Odyssey* supplies a model of poetic experience emphasizing that poetry offers its audience direct contact with the divine. In the Sirens episode we shall also find an answer to the question of how pleasure fits with divine knowledge in the Homeric conception of poetic experience. Is it simply that acquiring divine knowledge is itself a pleasurable experience? Does poetry's pleasure depend on its being an acquiring of knowledge otherwise forbidden to human beings?

---

[48] As we shall see in chapter 4, Socrates will deny that inspiration can convey divine knowledge, or any sort of knowledge at all.

The memorable and multilayered episode of the Sirens in Book 12 of the *Odyssey* represents the Homeric theory of poetic experience by exhibiting relations among poet, Muse, and audience to reveal, and at the same time to exploit, the link between pleasure and knowledge in poetic experience. There, by portraying knowledge as itself erotic, the Sirens exhibit Homer's theory at work *poetically,* attracting its auditors.

The Sirens

In Book 12 of the *Odyssey,* the Sirens seduce their victims with song and with the promise to share privileged knowledge of Troy.[49] They would consequently appear to serve as Homeric models of Muses or poets, and their effect on listeners would model the Homeric audiences' poetic experience. Yet adopting the Sirens scene as an allegory of poetic performance and reception immediately invites objection. The Sirens' treachery and fatal destructiveness has suggested to some commentators that, far from encouraging any model of poet and of the poetic experience of his audience, Homer portrays the Sirens as anti-poets and their song as anti-epic.[50] If applied to an audience's experience of Homeric poetry, the Siren model could also appear to clash with the interests of Homeric poetry by undermining the poem's claim to veracity. The Sirens are notorious deceivers, as their treacherous promise to "send their listener away" makes clear. Some current criticism concludes that the Sirens, unless they are clearly differentiated from Muses, leave no alternative to inferring that Homeric poetry too deceives its listener.[51] Both these considerations that appear to disqualify encounters with the Sirens as models for Homeric poetics are themselves deceptive. The theory that the Siren scene depicts is in fact the same theory we have already found repeated throughout the *Iliad* and *Odyssey.* With the Sirens Homer elaborates that theory by portraying its elements

---

[49] On the Sirens see Schadewalt 1965, p. 85; G. K. Gresseth, "The Homeric Sirens," *TAPA* 101 (1970), pp. 203–18; P. Pucci, "The Song of the Sirens," *Arethusa* 12 (1979), pp. 121–32 (reprinted in S. Schein, ed., *Reading the Odyssey* [Princeton, 1996], pp. 191–99); M. Blanchot, *The Sirens' Song* (Bloomington, 1982), pp. 59–65; P. Pucci, *Odysseus Polutropos: Intertextual Readings in the Odyssey and the Iliad* (Ithaca, 1987), pp. 209–13; S. W. De Rachewiltz, *De Sirenibus: An Inquiry into the Sirens from Homer to Shakespeare* (dissertation, Harvard University, 1987); C. Segal 1988, pp. 141–45; Goldhill 1991, pp. 64–65; Crotty 1994, p. 204; L. E. Doherty, "Sirens, Muses, and Female Narrators in the *Odyssey,*" in B. Cohen, ed., *The Distaff's Side: Representing the Female in Homer's Odyssey* (New York, 1995), pp. 81–92.

[50] See De Rachewiltz 1987, p. 37: ". . . the song of the Sirens is in some sense a counterfeit version, or enchanted mirror, of the epic storytelling of the bard, it seems at the same time to embody the problematic lure of something altogether Other."

[51] See Doherty 1995, pp. 83–89.

in further detail. The Siren model, we shall see, elaborates a Homeric view of the Muse as wielding an irresistibly powerful, and potentially devastating divine force; of the audience's poetic experience as an alluring, dangerous, and pleasurable acquiring of divine knowledge; and of the poet as provider of the means by which the audience can both directly encounter the divine power that the Sirens represent, and survive such a perilous encounter.

The Sirens, who claim to know "all the toils that in wide Troy the Argives and Trojans endured,"[52] boast to Odysseus of their twofold effect on a human audience. When a man has heard their song, they claim:

ἀλλ᾽ ὅ γε τερψάμενος νεῖται καὶ πλείονα εἰδώς.

then he goes away pleased and knowing more.

(12. 188)

The Sirens' promise, as we have seen, articulates the Homeric view that poetry's great allure weds knowledge to pleasure.[53] The Sirens specify that the knowledge their epic poetry conveys, of "all the toils that in wide Troy the Argives and Trojans endured," consists in information to which they are privileged. The Sirens conceal the fact that the combination of pleasure and knowledge that constitutes their song's allure holds peril. Their song, Circe has warned, has such an extraordinarily powerful effect that it paralyzes its auditor with desire so that he is left to die slowly as he listens to it: the Sirens so enchant men with their song that the beach before the meadow upon which they sit "is piled with boneheaps / of men now rotted away, and the skin shrivels upon them" (12. 45–46). In what does the devastating nature of the Siren's song consist? We are told explicitly only of its extraordinary *effect,* but the scene in fact discloses much about the nature of the cause as well.

The irresistible attraction of the Siren's song relies primarily on the suggestion of eroticism; the unavoidable and paralyzing desire incited by their song most obviously suggests sexual desire. This point has not been given the emphasis it deserves. To say merely that the Sirens represent the "seductive powers of song" underplays the role of the erotic in Homer's model of poetry.[54] The Sirens' eroticism, evoking a familiar connection with the

---

[52] *Odyssey* 12. 189–90.

[53] Cicero *De Finibus* 5. 18, recognized that in Homer's depiction of the Sirens it is the pleasure men take in learning that attracts them to the Sirens: *Neque enim vocum suavitate videntur aut novitate quadam et varietate cantandi revocare eos solitae qui praetervehebantur, sed quia multa se scire profitebantur, ut homines ad earum saxa discendi cupiditate adhaerescerent.*

[54] De Rachewiltz 1987, p. 34; cf. also Doherty's (1985, p. 88) hesitant formulation (italics mine): "[The Sirens] are *potentially* sexual, but narrative, not sex, is the true source of their power." What, then, lies at the source of *narrative*'s great power?

threat of death, excludes poetry from the ranks of the benignly seductive. Poetry's divine transmission of divine knowledge holds potential perils for its audience, as the Sirens' fatal attractiveness demonstrates. In this respect the Sirens naturally invite comparison to Calypso and Circe, who each (posing a threat of their own) sing poetry as part of successful attempts to seduce,[55] and to Helen, who unites treacherous sexual appeal with her role as poet-figure.[56] Odysseus's encounter with the Sirens, however, includes a striking feature that underscores the emblematic connections the scene makes between desire, knowledge, and the visual. Unlike other representations of the Sirens in Greek art and literature, Homer's includes no visual description; the whole scene is in fact depicted in almost purely auditory terms.[57] The purely auditory nature of the Sirens' initial contact with the listener seduces through withholding the visual. This withholding of the visual, specifically of the female body or object of desire, focuses the scene's interest on eroticism and anticipates modern narrative's pattern of representing those bodies most desired as those most unavailable for viewing, or for full viewing.[58] Furthermore, by explicitly connecting this withholding of the visual with the more general promise of knowledge, the scene dramatizes the psychoanalytic model at the basis of modern realist narrative's positing "the body held in the field of vision" as "par excellence the object of both knowing and desire, knowing as desire, desire as knowing."[59] According to the Freudian model, the desire to know as such originates in the child's desire to see the anatomical distinction between the sexes—a desire inevitably frustrated and so fixated on an imaginary object.[60] The

---

[55] Circe at *Odyssey* 10. 220–22: "[Odysseus and his companions] stood there in the forecourt of the goddess with the glorious hair, and heard Circe inside singing in a sweet voice as she went up and down a great design on a loom . . . " (cf. 224–31); Calypso at *Odyssey* 5. 61–62: "She was singing inside the cave with a sweet voice as she went up and down the loom and wove with a golden shuttle."

[56] For Helen's metaphorical poetry making, see *Iliad* 3. 125–28. Cf. Austin 1994, pp. 37–41.

[57] De Rachewiltz 1987, p. 23, notes that "sight is almost banished from this episode . . . even distances are given in auditory terms—'But when we were as far from the land as a voice shouting carries' (12. 181–182), and further on '. . . when we could no longer hear their voices and lost the sound of their singing . . . ' (12. 197–98). Though the Sirens see the ship, Odysseus does not mention seeing them at any point. Tied upright to the mast, he is literally 'all ears'; like a sail filled by the wind, he stretches out to receive the 'full blast' of the magic song, while his companions duck as they bend over the oars." For visual representations of the Sirens, see T. Gantz, *Early Greek Myth: A Guide to Literary and Artistic Sources* (Baltimore and London, 1993), pp. 150, 708–9.

[58] P. Brooks, *Body Work: Objects of Desire in Modern Narrative* (Cambridge, 1993); on Helen in this regard, see N. Worman, "The Body as Argument: Helen in Four Greek Texts," *Classical Antiquity* 16 (1997), pp. 151–203.

[59] Brooks 1993, p. 99.

[60] Brooks 1993, pp. 9–10; 99–100.

episode of the Sirens would seem to demonstrate this connection between sexuality and the desire to know in general, as it links the male's desire for the Sirens' apparently unlimited knowledge with his particular erotic attraction to thêm. In particular, this scene's withholding of any visual description of the Sirens makes it unmistakable that, in addition to the actual auditory object of Odysseus's desire, there exists an imaginary visual object as well.

The striking similarity between the Sirens and Muses has often been noted.[61] Both are female divinities whose power and primary activity is song. Yet what the Sirens' song conveys fatally paralyzes its auditors. As we have seen, Homer portrays the poet as a conduit of the Muses' divine power; does the poet subject his audience to the fatal danger the Sirens so vividly represent? In that case, the Sirens would stand for poets, and poets would convey divine power devastating to human beings. This implication, among others, has led some commentators to deny that Sirens stand for Muses.[62] I would suggest, however, that Homeric poetics provides an alternative to disregarding the Sirens' and Muses' manifest similarities of status and role.

It is Circe, not the Sirens, who allegorically portrays the poet in the Siren episode. Circe was previously introduced as a poet-figure when Odysseus and his companions entered her palace and heard her enchanting singing.[63] She continues in the same role in the Siren scene, I would suggest, where she dramatizes the poet's ability to afford his audience a direct, perceptual experience of the divine. Circe contributes by arming Odysseus and his companions with means of escaping the fate of all the humans who have listened to the Sirens. She instructs Odysseus to plug his companions' ears with wax. By shielding them from the divine power that the Sirens communicate, this protection excludes the companions from the Sirens' audience. Circe's instructions for Odysseus himself ensure that he, unlike his companions, can experience the power of Sirens' song undiminished by mute or filter. By binding himself to his ship's mast, Odysseus may both experience the full power of the Sirens' song and escape the fate of the corpses on the beach. As Odysseus in this familiar scene is the audience, so the poet is Circe, and the Sirens, despite their fatal effect on all unprotected auditors, may be said to stand for Muses.

Homer makes clear enough that we should think of what he contributes as poet as in part similar to Circe's contribution to Odysseus's surviving his encounter with the Sirens. To discover just what Homer would have us think a poet contributes, we may look to Circe, who arms Odysseus with

---

[61] See, e.g., Pucci 1979; Doherty 1995, p. 83.
[62] See, e.g., Doherty 1995, pp. 83–89.
[63] *Odyssey* 10. 220–22.

practical instructions about the use of specific materials that enable him to survive his encounter with the full divine power of the Sirens.[64] The poet's skill, we are to infer, enables him to make safe, but avoid adulterating, the knowledge transmitted to his audience from the divine source; like Circe's, the poet's mediation makes possible direct contact with the divine.[65]

As we have seen, Homer elsewhere portrays the poet as a passive conveyor of divine inspiration, as the prophet through whom the Muses speak. A general issue is raised, then, of whether Homer divides the poet's contribution into two factors: the prophetic function of communicating to his audience divine knowledge and a separate art of lending voice to the divine communication (that is, the poet's skill). The division of the poet's contribution into two factors, both craftsman and seer, may be supposed to correspond to the bard Phemius's well-known characterization of himself: "I sing to the gods and to human people, and I am taught by myself, but the god has inspired me in the song-ways of every kind."[66] Homer leaves indeterminate, and so could be seen as conflating, the relationship between the poet's functions as craftsman and as prophet. This indeterminacy will prove important when we come to Socratic poetics. We will also find that Socrates pursues two questions that remain about the poet's skill: what is the nature of the poet's mediating power? Has he a *technê* by which he commands what he conveys in verse? Insofar as a self-taught ability must be presumed unteachable to others, the poet's skill, on the Homeric view, would appear to count as something less than mastery or knowledge or a *technê*.

The Sirens' fatal danger, then, does not prevent them from standing for Muses in a model of Homeric poetics. Yet a second difficulty remains in the way of accepting the Sirens as proxies for Muses. The Sirens' role as deceivers of men apparently conflicts with the truth claims of epic discourse and therefore with the Muses' claims to convey knowledge. The Sirens' duplicity has suggested to some commentators that, far from encouraging their identification with Muses, Homer should be understood to emphasize the differences between Sirens and Muses and in this way to seek to contain this threat against the authority of his own work.[67] I would sug-

---

[64] Compare Calypso's giving Odysseus the technical knowledge of how to build a raft (*Odyssey* 5. 162–64).

[65] I cannot, then, agree with Ford 1992, p. 85, who sees Odysseus as the poet-figure in this episode. Odysseus is here manifestly an *audience,* and as such invites Homer's audience to identify with his pleasurable and alluringly dangerous experience. Contrast also Ford's account of the poet's mediation as setting limits to the limitless tradition (pp. 83–86).

[66] *Odyssey* 22. 346–48: . . . ὅς τε θεοῖσι καὶ ἀνθρώποισιν ἀείδω. / αὐτοδίδακτος δ᾿ εἰμί, θεὸς δέ μοι ἐν φρεσὶν οἴμας / παντοίας ἐνέφυσεν·

[67] Drawing on Pucci's work, Doherty 1995, p. 83–84, claims that "Taken to its logical conclusion, the equation between Sirens and Muses would have the effect of subverting the poet's authority by hinting at the seductive aspects of his own activity."

gest, alternatively, that Homer's implicitly attributing to the Muses the power to deceive need not threaten the poet's authority nor undermine his promise to convey knowledge. For Homer, the Sirens' portrayal of the Muses' capacity for deception boasts of the divine power at poetry's source and reminds the audience of our dependence on the gods for such knowledge as we have. Homer focuses, we have seen, on the power to *supply* knowledge, not on the power to withhold it, but the two are indeed inseparable.[68] We shall see that Homeric poetics differs from its Hesiodic counterpart, which exploits for very different results the Muses' power to deceive. Homer does not require us to adopt a skeptical position about his poetry, as we shall see that Hesiod does.

Similarly, Homer's depiction of others—most notably Odysseus—as poet-figures who routinely deceive does nothing to threaten the authority of epic discourse.[69] On the contrary, it illustrates how singers like Odysseus, who lack a connection to the Muses, may use impressive powers of representation as they wish, to convey the truth or to deceive. Odysseus's role as poet-figure is well established and widely illustrated. After hearing Odysseus's moving tale, Alcinoos remarks that Odysseus sings "knowledgeably" (ἐπισταμένως), like a bard.[70] So too, Eumaios says that his guest enchants like a singer.[71] In the climactic moment when Odysseus strings his bow in preparation to taking vengeance on the suitors, Homer compares him to a skillful bard stringing his lyre.[72] More subtle, but all the more poignant comparisons occur when Odysseus speaks to Nausicaa in language that is uncharacteristic for him, but not for the Homeric narrator,[73] and when at 9. 19ff. Odysseus articulates a decidedly out of character, bardic view of *kleos* by introducing himself as Odysseus, who is "known before all men for the study of crafty designs" and whose "fame goes up to heaven."[74]

From several points of view it would be problematic to infer that, through his characterization of Odysseus as a deceiver, Homer represents the poet—and thus himself—as a deceiver. The poem firmly distinguishes Odysseus from the genuine poet by omitting to depict him in any relation to the Muses—the source of the poet's power. Without such a connection

---

[68] For Plato, of course, if the source can deceive (as the senses can), then one cannot get knowledge from it; but it would be anachronistic to attribute that Platonic assumption to Homer. The thought in Homer rather seems to be that whether or not something is known is dependent on external sources.

[69] The picture of Odysseus as a poet-figure who lies eloquently and persuasively is thought to suggest that poetry is, or can itself be, a source of deception rather than truth (Hesiod's Muses, who can tell the truth or lies resembling the truth are often cited here). E.g., Thalmann 1984, p. 172; Goldhill 1991, p. 67; Walsh 1984, p. 20; Pratt 1993, pp. 55–94.

[70] *Odyssey* 11. 368.

[71] *Odyssey* 17. 512–21.

[72] *Odyssey* 21. 406.

[73] *Odyssey* 6. 149–52. See Goldhill 1991, p. 67.

[74] See Segal 1988, pp. 138–39.

to the supernatural, Odysseus lacks at least one credential essential for a Homeric poet. Specific features of Odysseus's narratives distinguish them from the poet's, such as Odysseus's failure to give specific references to divinities.[75] Still, the comparisons of Odysseus to the poet retain full significance, because the poet is of course among the roles Odysseus portrays. As the man who is *polutropos,* Odysseus enacts a seemingly universal array of experiences,[76] and outstanding among his leading roles is his portrayal of the poet. Odysseus is not a poet, but his success at playing the part is illustrated by the way other characters in the poem respond to him. To say, then, that Homer dramatizes himself through the figure of Odysseus obscures the complexity of artistic representation. Homer does not represent himself through the character of Odysseus, rather, he represents Odysseus skillfully playing the part of the poet. In one of his roles as a master of disguise, Odysseus ultimately emerges in contrast to the truly inspired Homeric bard. Unlike the inspired bard whose connection to the divine guarantees his poetry's veracity, Odysseus's great powers of representation carry no such assurance. Comparisons of Odysseus with the poet, then, focus on displaying Odysseus's multifaceted character. They contribute to a Homeric theory of the poet only by way of contrast.

Although the Sirens' fatal treachery may at first discourage our taking this episode to model Homeric poetics, these features actually lure the reader with an enchanting model of poetic experience, and contribute to making the theory all the more bold and enticing. With the Sirens as surrogates for Muses, Odysseus as audience, and Circe portraying the poet, this sexualized episode dramatizes Homeric poetic theory. The Sirens' portrayal of Muses links poetry essentially with a divine knowledge fused with erotic pleasure.[77] The Sirens themselves explicitly draw this connection by promising their listener pleasure *and* knowledge. The Sirens' erotic attraction could eclipse any other of Odysseus's thoughts or memories. But it is knowledge/pleasure rather than forgetfulness that the Homeric theory emphasizes.[78] Here we must again anticipate the contrast of Homer's theory with Hesiodic poetics' emphasis on poetry as relief from workaday cares.[79]

[75] See J. S. Clay, *The Wrath of Athena* (Princeton, 1983), pp. 21–25.

[76] See Thalmann 1984, p. 174.

[77] Thus I cannot agree with Finkelberg, who assumes that since knowledge in Homer is associated with that class of activities for which man is held responsible, we must conclude that all knowledge associated with poetry refers to some technical skill for which the poet has responsibility, like lyre playing, for example, and not to that domain for which the Muses are given credit (see Finkelberg 1998, ch. 2). The passages I have discussed challenge Finkelberg's assumption. As Circe's role illustrates, the poet indeed has a skill; but he also conveys to his audience the Muses' divine, quasi-perceptual knowledge of epic events (not some craft-knowledge or skill).

[78] Contrast Walsh 1984, pp. 14–15.

[79] As I will discuss in the next chapter.

By (as it were) eroticizing the epistemological, the Sirens suggest that poetry conveys knowledge with the immediacy and pleasure associated with sense experience. This result, together with the structure of invocation we have examined and the suggestive rhetoric of other passages, enforces an Auerbachean notion of poetry as providing perceptual data and discouraging any notions that Homer would allow his poetry to stand in need of interpretation or to invite critical evaluation. It is also noteworthy that a distinction between knowledge and understanding does not figure into the Homeric conception of poetic knowledge. The poet promises the audience knowledge issuing from a divine authority's grasp of an independent object of its sense perception for which the issue of interpretation never arises. There is no suggestion in the theory, then, that the meaning of poetry is equivocal and in need of clarification or illumination, no suggestion that the audience might, after engaging in a process of interpretation, arrive at an *understanding* of it.[80] Knowledge, according to the theory, is conveyed just as a result of hearing the inspired poet's song.

Does the Theory Apply to the Poem?

Homer dramatizes some episodes that do not fit his theory of what an audience's poetic experience should be. In each of these episodes, characters within the poem stand in a unique historical relation to the events in the poem. Both Odysseus and Penelope, for example, react to poetry with pain and anguish because of their personal involvement with the stories the poet relates. Odysseus weeps when, as a guest of the Phaeacians, he hears the bard Demodocus sing of the sufferings at Troy.[81] Penelope weeps as she is reminded of Odysseus by Phemius's song, and her reaction serves as the catalyst for Telemachus's seizure of authority.[82] Commentators have in general taken Odysseus's and Penelope's reactions as models of poetic response.[83] Some have seen depicted here an alternative psychology of the Homeric audience which creates an unresolved contradiction in Homer's notion of art and poetic truth.[84] According to Walsh, the Homeric view has poetry normally convey a pleasant and enchanting truth that avoids di-

---

[80] Contrast Crotty 1994, pp. 183–204. Crotty (p. 183) may be correct to see examples of obscure speech and the need for interpretation in the relationship and conversations between Odysseus and Penelope in the *Odyssey,* but there is no compelling reason to take these, as Crotty does, as Homer's models for the nature of poetry.

[81] *Odyssey* 8. 521–34.

[82] *Odyssey* 1. 328–44.

[83] On models of the audience and poetic response in Homer see especially Redfield 1973, pp. 150–53; Macleod 1983, p. 11; Thalmann 1984, pp. 159–60; Murnaghan 1987, p. 151; Goldhill 1991, pp. 58–9; Segal 1992, p. 10.

[84] Walsh 1984, pp. 3–21.

rectly addressing the audience's experience and diverts them from the concerns of their own lives. Odysseus and Penelope illustrate poetry that is exceptional because its truths excite painful memories of their own experiences. The reactions of Odysseus and Penelope, on this view, illustrate an alternative Homeric account of poetic experience, where poetry can bring audiences no diversion from their painful experience, but engages directly with the experience of the listener. Others have seen in Odysseus's and Penelope's reactions not merely an alternative psychology, but a Homeric prototype for the ideal, "mature" response to poetry, which discerns poetry's connection to real experience.[85] The mature response, on Thalmann's view, contrasts with the immature responses he finds in Telemachus and Alcinoos, who each respond solely to poetry's artistic value and aesthetic charms. On this interpretation, Odysseus and Penelope respond to poetry optimally because each takes poetry seriously, not as entertainment and diversion, but as ingredients in the central experiences of their lives.

If Odysseus's and Penelope's reactions to song do model poetic response, then we must take into account their implications for the Homeric view of poetic experience. I would suggest, however, that their reactions are not in fact examples of specifically *poetic* response. Penelope and Odysseus respond not to poetry as such, but to associated memories that poetry merely triggers. The poetry they hear happens to have memorial significance for them since they are in the exceptional position of being among the very subjects of that poetry. These characters within the heroic world hear poetry in which they figure as characters, not as audience. Because Penelope and Odysseus are themselves part of the poem's subject matter, their response to poetry is nonpoetic. The historical significance this poetry holds for them intrudes to prevent them from having poetic experience. The poem relies on just this breakdown of poetic experience to lend these scenes much of their dramatic effectiveness. Penelope, for example, cannot respond to Phemius's song as poetry because it cannot offer her knowledge of any world different from her own. The poetic world represented by Phemius's song is the actual world of Penelope's own memory, so its actuality prevents her from having a poetic experience. It is not that Penelope (and Odysseus when he weeps at Demodocus's songs) illustrates an alternative model of poetic experience, but rather that her response illustrates an extraordinary situation where poetic experience is thwarted: poetry offers to most audiences an experience that, as Homer urges, is like

---

[85] Thalmann 1984, p. 159; Redfield 1973, p. 150. See also Macleod 1983, p. 11, who sees Odysseus's grieving response to poetry as a model for Homeric poetry that shows that to hear poetry can be to "understand that suffering belongs to all men, and so too to learn to live with our own." So too Segal 1992, p. 10, argues that Odysseus's response to Demodocus articulates a model of response that reveals the "paradox of the pleasure art affords through suffering."

perceptual experience. For Penelope it can only prompt memory. In her case, memory experience subverts Homeric poetic experience.

Penelope's own remarks bear out this interpretation. She dismisses the bard Phemius, explaining that his song afflicts her with grief because it reminds her of her husband ("So dear a head do I long for whenever I am reminded [μεμνημένη]/ of my husband," [343–44]). The song has triggered Penelope's memory; she responds not to the song, but to what it causes her to recollect—viz., her own longing for her husband. Just because she recognizes her experience as memory, the song cannot transport her as poetic experience typically does. Rather, Homer dramatizes a kind of breakdown in the usual mechanism of poetic response: what for the typical audience is a poetic experience, is for her a reminder. Penelope's response to poetry, then, cannot illustrate Homer's audience's experience because, unlike them, her recollection excludes the quasi-perceptual experience that is Homeric poetic experience.

Telemachus's response to his mother need not reflect an immature or superficial attitude to poetry. On the contrary, it may accuse *Penelope*, with justification, of immaturity or self-centeredness:

μῆτερ ἐμή, τί τ' ἄρα φθονέεις ἐρίηρον ἀοιδὸν
τέρπειν ὅππῃ οἱ νόος ὄρνυται; οὔ νύ τ' ἀοιδοὶ
αἴτιοι, ἀλλά ποθι Ζεὺς αἴτιος, ὅς τε δίδωσιν
ἀνδράσιν ἀλφηστῇσιν ὅπως ἐθέλῃσιν ἑκάστῳ.
τούτῳ δ' οὐ νέμεσις Δαναῶν κακὸν οἶτον ἀείδειν·
τὴν γὰρ ἀοιδὴν μᾶλλον ἐπικλείουσ' ἄνθρωποι,
ἥ τις ἀκουόντεσσι νεωτάτη ἀμφιπέληται.
σοὶ δ' ἐπιτολμάτω κραδίη καὶ θυμὸς ἀκούειν·
οὐ γὰρ Ὀδυσσεὺς οἶος ἀπώλεσε νόστιμον ἦμαρ
ἐν Τροίῃ, πολλοὶ δὲ καὶ ἄλλοι φῶτες ὄλοντο.

Why, my mother, do you begrudge this excellent singer
his pleasing himself as the thought drives him? It is not the singers
who are to blame, it must be Zeus is to blame, who gives out
to men who eat bread, to each and all, the way he wills it.
There is nothing wrong in his singing the sad return of the Danaans.
People, surely, always give more applause to that song
which is the latest to circulate among the listeners.
So let your heart and let your spirit be hardened to listen.
Odysseus is not the only one who lost his homecoming
day at Troy. There were many others who perished, beside him.

(1. 346–55)

Telemachus shows every sign of understanding Penelope's reaction to hearing Phemius's song. He does not berate her for remembering and grieving for Odysseus, but only for ordering Phemius to stop singing. On Telemachus's view, Penelope should bear her grief for the sake of others who are able to have a genuine poetic experience. So it is not Penelope's response to the poem to which Telemachus objects, but the action she takes on the basis of her response. There is no indication that Telemachus views song as mere amusement, or that he is not himself reminded of his father—only that, unlike Penelope, he chooses to act on behalf of the others, who presumably are not prevented by troubling memories from enjoying poetic experience as the Homeric theory defines it. If anything, Penelope's actions are viewed here as the less mature, since according to her son, she thinks primarily of herself and exaggerates the peculiarity of her situation. Still, in a different respect, the main idea that comes across is Penelope's exceptional status as an audience. Penelope is not unique, since others (within the heroic world) are vulnerable to unpleasant memories triggered by Phemius's song. Yet on this occasion she is the exception. Ironically, it is at a moment when she is viewed critically by her son that Homer emphasizes her heroic status: only for characters within the heroic world—and not for the external audience—can poetry trigger the sort of memory experience it does for Penelope. For the external audience, heroic experience seems that much more remote. The case of Penelope shows, then, how for her and Odysseus, poetry can be the occasion for a memory experience that interferes with their having a genuinely *poetic* experience. Because in these instances Penelope and Odysseus are prevented from responding to poetry as such, their responses should be counted as *contrasting* with the Homeric theory of poetic response. The breakdown of poetic experience makes these scenes all the more striking and moving in their portrayals of human suffering.

We can now turn to the more general question of the extent to which Homeric poetics provides a fully adequate theory of the Homeric poems themselves. To what extent do the poems conform to the Homeric theory? Auerbach claimed to have identified a pervasive feature of Homeric narrative that discourages audiences from interpretation. Do the poems effectively discourage their audience from interpreting, as Auerbach claimed? What of the distinguished work of so much interpretive Homeric scholarship? Can the *Iliad* and *Odyssey* only be misinterpreted?

We have already mentioned some objections that have been raised to Auerbach's reading of Homer, for example, to his interpretation of the scar scene and, more generally, to his claim that Homeric narrative lacks perspective, background, and indeterminacies of meaning.[86] We may add to these the observation that the passages dealing with poetry themselves seem to violate their own antitheoretical promptings. The Sirens episode

---

[86] See note 7.

in particular, which both exhibits and alluringly commends a perceptual model of poetic knowledge, at the same time appears to contradict the theory it depicts by encouraging Homer's audience to identify with Odysseus, our fellow auditor of the poet's song. We thus enter the action of the poem just where it illustrates the audience's part as unreflective perceiver of its action. The invocation to the catalogue of ships in *Iliad* 2 still more blatantly draws the audience into the poem with its reference to and characterization of "us" mortals.

Another passage raises further complexities. When in Book 8 of the *Odyssey* the Phaeacian bard Demodocus sings the story of Ares and Aphrodite, Odysseus enjoys it because, unlike Demodocus's other two songs, (the story of Odysseus's quarrel with Achilles and the tale of the Trojan horse) this tale offers him undiluted diversion. Taken as it relates to Odysseus as audience this song serves as a model of poetic experience consistent with the Homeric theory we have found articulated repeatedly: the poem opens to him a window onto another world. And yet, insofar as Odysseus serves as an audience-figure, this scene too encourages Homer's audience to identify with him. It thus violates the Auerbachean principle of Homeric poetics, that the epic world excludes its audience. Moreover, for Homer's audience, the song resonates with any number of implied meanings. Its relevance to the immediate context in Phaeacia as well as its bearing on the situation in Ithaca has been shown to emerge in particular through the parallels between Hephaistos and Odysseus.[87] It has also been suggested that through this tale's parallels with the situation involving Penelope and the suitors in Ithaca, Homer manipulates his audience's interpretation of that situation and ultimately their response to Odysseus's slaying of the suitors.[88]

The resonances of Demodocus's song—the same sort that can arguably be found in much of Homeric poetry—may be said to invite intratextual interpretation, that is, the inferring of meanings drawn from connections made among passages or episodes within the Homeric text. We have also seen ways that the poems point beyond the limits of the text to invite readers to see themselves as related to its structures of meaning; the passages dealing with poetry (paradoxically) invite just the sort of theorizing that Homeric poetics would suppress. Other general truths have been said to emerge from the *Iliad* or *Odyssey* as a whole (for example, the *Iliad* as an anti-war poem, or as a poem about human compassion), and from any number of passages. The Homeric poems, then, would unavoidably seem to invite the very sort of interpretation discouraged by Homeric poetics.

---

[87] See *Odyssey* 8. 266–369; G. P. Rose, *The Song of Ares and Aphrodite* (Ph.D. dissertation, Berkeley, 1969), pp. 6–14 ; R. M. Newton, "Odysseus and Hephaestus in the *Odyssey*," *CJ* 83 (1987), pp. 12–20.

[88] M. J. Alden, "The Resonances of the Song of Ares and Aphrodite," *Mnemosyne* 50 (1997), pp. 513–29.

This result for the theory poses a limitation only for Homer as a theorist. I have suggested instead that we view Homer's poetics finally as a contribution to advancing his poetic ends. Homer's theory can achieve its poetic ends despite theoretical limitations. Although the passages presenting the theory invite the reader to interpret and to think theoretically, their *poetic* (nontheoretical) form—to the extent that it successfully draws the reader into the fullness of its own detail—discourages the reader's thought from remaining theoretical and works to lure them back from the discursive into the quasi-perceptual mode. The reader is thereby diverted from evaluating the theory's adequacy as a theory applicable to the poem—as she all the while is being enchanted by the theory's conception of poetic experience.

By setting out a compelling theory of poetry that promises divine knowledge and discourages interpretation, Homer issues an implicit challenge to his rivals and successors who face tasks of fashioning their own compelling poetics under his unavoidable influence. As we shall see, both Hesiod and Pindar respond to this challenge with theories that are innovative and yet, in different ways, reenact Homer's own attempt to preserve authority for the poet by forestalling interpretation.

Chapter Two

Hesiod's Naturalism

THE HOMERIC POEMS promise their audience supernatural knowledge. Such a grandiose undertaking leaves them vulnerable to criticism that Homer endeavored to deflect. Xenophanes, and later Plato, famously criticize both Homer and Hesiod for portraying the gods as immoral.[1] Heraclitus's charge that Hesiod and others possessed "learning of many things" (*polumathia*) rather than intelligence views poetry through the lens of Homeric poetics and turns that theory against itself. The charge of *polumathia* amounts to the charge that a certain kind of poetry amasses and conveys information, but does not lead us toward true understanding of the *logos*, which would require interpretation.[2] As we shall see, this is not the only time that the particular type of knowledge exploited by Homeric poetics will be criticized as an inadequate conception of knowledge. The Homeric theory may indeed contribute to the enchanting nature of Homeric poetry, but when its claim to provide knowledge comes to be assessed philosophically, it must compete with rival conceptions of knowledge. So too, the Homeric poems are open to charges of immorality precisely because they purport to offer nothing less than *knowledge*—a definitive and authoritative account of their subject matter, secure against all challenges. Hesiod's *Theogony* may also appear vulnerable in this regard, since it graphically depicts the gods engaging in cannibalism, violence, and deception. As we shall see, however, Hesiod's poetics effectively insulates his poem against such censure. Like Homer's poetics, Hesiod's theory of poetry holds that all knowledge of his poem's subject matter is divine knowledge. But unlike Homer's, Hesiod's theory embraces and exploits a kind of skepticism. According to his theory, neither the poet nor his audience can know whether what poetry conveys is true. The source of the poet's gift is divine,

---

[1] Xenophanes DK 22 B 11 refers specifically to theft, adultery, and deception; Plato *Republic* 377e–383c to deception, to the gods' being the cause of anything bad, and to the gods' inconstancy of appearance. As we shall see in the next chapter, Pindar belongs in this tradition as well.

[2] Heraclitus DK 22 B 40 does not mention Homer explicitly: Πολυμαθίη νόον ἔχειν οὐ διδάσκει· Ἡσίοδον γὰρ ἂν ἐδίδαξε καὶ Πυθαγόρην αὖτίς τε Ξενοφάνεά τε καὶ Ἑκαταῖον ("Learning of many things does not teach intelligence; if so it would have taught Hesiod and Pythagoras, and again Xenophanes and Hecataeus."). But his remarks at DK 22 B 42 may imply that the charge of *polumathia* applies to Homer as well. See Kahn's discussion in *The Art and Thought of Heraclitus,* pp. 107–10.

but does not let him know whether his poetry relates truths or falsehoods. Unlike Homer, therefore, it is not knowledge that Hesiod can offer to share with his audience, even though his poem may contain truths. By disavowing that he is engaging in moral pedagogy, Hesiod preempts objections on grounds of inaccuracy.[3] Skepticism, we shall see, allows Hesiod to avoid the Homeric poet's role of divinely knowledgeable instructor of his audience and to draw attention instead to the poet as benefactor and healer of human ills. Hesiod's poet aims primarily at the practical, therapeutic end of relieving problems of the human psyche. The *Theogony* encourages this view of the poet as focused on his power to benefit human beings in their mundane condition. While the Homeric poet addresses his audience as potential receivers of divine knowledge, Hesiod's addresses them as patients.[4]

Hesiodic skepticism, I shall argue, contributes to a poetics that contrasts with Homeric poetic's avowed supernaturalism. Nevertheless, it has been said that Hesiod's account of poetry is more supernatural than Homer's.[5] That claim has the ring of truth when we consider that the proem to the *Theogony* pictures its poet's power as born of a supernatural encounter. The Muses appear to Hesiod as he tends his flocks. Their speech breaths into him a divine voice that invests in the shepherd his power to sing. A general critical disposition also supports this claim. Viewing Hesiodic thought as the more primitive tends to encourage treatment of Hesiodic poetics as immersed in an elemental religious experience. Compared to the Homeric bards Phemius and Demodocus, for example, Hesiod does represent himself less realistically and more detached from the earthly context of performing song. Indeed, on this view the scene of Hesiod's initiation, although filled with tangible details of his encounter with the Muses, also appears to be a transaction on an ethereal plane, where gods interact freely and openly with mortals. Hesiod's self-portrait omits any further glimpse

---

[3] This may explain why the *Theogony* contains and *Works and Days* omits a poetics: the *Works and Days* does not attribute morally controversial behavior to the gods. There, far from disavowing moral pedagogy, the narrator's posture is explicitly didactic.

[4] On various aspects of Hesiod's poetics see: J.-P. Vernant, "Aspects mythique de la mémoire et du temps," in Vernant 1965a, pp. 80–107; Detienne 1967, p. 8ff.; Harriott 1969, pp. 10–36; Svenbro 1976, pp. 46–73; P. Pucci, *Hesiod and the Language of Poetry* (Baltimore, 1977); M. Arthur, "The Dream of a World Without Women: Poetics and the Circles of Order in the *Theogony* Prooemium," *Arethusa* 16 (1983), pp. 97–135; Walsh 1984, pp. 22–36; Thalmann 1984, pp. 134–56; J. S. Clay, "What the Muses Sang: *Theogony* 1–115," *Greek, Roman and Byzantine Studies* 29 (1988), pp. 323–33; G. Ferrari, "Hesiod's Mimetic Muses and the Strategies of Deconstruction," in A. Benjamin, ed., *Post-Structuralist Classics* (London and New York, 1988), pp. 45–78; J. Kirby, "Rhetoric and Poetics in Hesiod," *Ramus* 21 (1992), pp. 34–60; R. Martin, "Hesiod's Metanastic Poetics," *Ramus* 21 (1992), pp. 11–33; Pratt 1993, pp. 95–113.

[5] Segal 1992, p. 28.

of the bard as he appears in the mortal world, so the idea remains fixed that his poem communicates his privileged connection with divinity. I shall show, however, how this view contradicts Hesiod's own conception of the poet. Hesiod conceives of the poet not as supernaturally gifted with the power to transmit the Muses' superhuman knowledge, but as *emulating* the Muses, whose divine performances entertain the gods with song. For Hesiod, the poet's relation to the divine is thus mimetic. Although he does claim a divine source for his poetic gift, Hesiod's poetics ensures that the poet's power, like its products, is itself mundane.[6]

Poetry and Skepticism

The proem to the *Theogony* serves as an extended meditation on the nature of poetry and the poet's art. Striking in its complexity and arresting in its disclosure of the poet's personality,[7] this invocation contrasts with its Homeric counterpart's more oblique representations of poet and Muse. The structural intricacy of these 115 lines suggests many ways of dividing the proem into sections whose multivalent relations contribute to the rich texture of Hesiodic poetics. But a general division of the proem into two sections bears most directly on the substance of Hesiod's view of the poet's function and his relation to the Muses. Both sections, (1) lines 1–35 and (2) lines 36–115, announce beginnings that align symmetrically by the parallel language of their first lines:

Μουσάων Ἑλικωνιάδων ἀρχώμεθ' ἀείδειν

From the Muses of Helicon let us begin our singing (1)

Τύνη, Μουσάων ἀρχώμεθα, . . .

Come now, from the Muses let us begin . . . (36)

These two sections, I shall show, divide the Muses' contribution from the poet's, and elaborate details of a specific relation between the two.

The focus of the first section sharpens towards the end as Hesiod describes his encounter with the Muses on Mount Helicon. The Muses and the poet are each pictured in vivid images, the Muses as divine singers and dancers, and Hesiod as lowly shepherd. The poet's report of the Muses' striking address has sparked some vigorous scholarly debate:

---

[6] It is worth noting a temporal factor that contributes to Hesiod's naturalism. Hesiod undergoes a supernatural encounter with Muses, but he represents himself as a poet from his audience's own time. Homer's bards, by contrast, are members of the heroic age and so that much closer to the immortal gods.

[7] I examine the issue of personality below.

ποιμένες ἄγραυλοι, κάκ' ἐλέγχεα, γαστέρες οἶον,
ἴδμεν ψεύδεα πολλὰ λέγειν ἐτύμοισιν ὁμοῖα,
ἴδμεν δ', εὖτ' ἐθέλωμεν, ἀληθέα γηρύσασθαι.

Shepherds whose home is in the wilds, disgraces to your trade,
    mere bellies,
We know how to tell many falsehoods that seem real:
but we also know how to speak the truth when we wish to.

(26–28)

Hesiod goes on to report that the Muses presented him with a staff made from a laurel branch and "breathed into" him a divine voice (αὐδὴν θέσπιν, 31–32) so that he might sing his theogony. The section concludes with a dismissive proverbial remark that oddly disparages the previous thirty-five lines: "But enough of this gossiping" (ἀλλὰ τίη μοι ταῦτα περὶ δρῦν ἢ περὶ πέτρην, 35). The poet begins anew in line 36, invoking the Muses once again, as if to start the proem all over again.

The Muses' provocative remarks in lines 27–28 raise pressing questions. Why, for example, should the poem introduce the possibility that the divine source of its poetry lacks veracity? How can deceitful Muses advance the poet's aim to build anticipation and promote the importance of his own enterprise? Why should the poet subvert his audience's belief that they are to be offered accurate information in the poem that follows?

The majority of commentators find it unacceptable that Hesiod should undermine his poetry as these questions suggest he does. The standard view maintains that, with the Muses' words, Hesiod indirectly denounces falsehood in his *rivals'* poetry (Homer's in particular), and claims true discourse as the exclusive privilege of his own poetry.[8] One objection occasionally raised against this interpretation is not decisive; it cites verses 44–52 and 99–101 to show that Hesiod considers heroic narrative on a par with his own poetry.[9] There, the Muses' song is said to include songs of "mankind" and "the glorious deeds of men in former times," so it would appear to include epic. The standard view need not claim, however, that heroic narrative *necessarily* consists of falsehoods, only that not all poets—composers of heroic narrative included—enjoy a connection to the Muses that guarantees the truth of their poetry. The Muses' boast of their power to either deceive or tell the truth, then, would not draw a generic distinc-

[8] See, e.g., Sikes 1931, pp. 5–6; W. Luther, *Wahrheit und Lüge* (Leipzig, 1935), pp. 124–26; K. Latte, "Hesiods Dichterweihe," *Antike und Abendland* 2 (1946), p. 159; W. J. Verdenius, "Notes on the Proem of Hesiod's *Theogony*," *Mnemosyne* 25 (1972), p. 234; Murray 1981, p. 91; Puelma 1989, pp. 74–79.

[9] See H. Koller, "Das kitharodische Prooimion," *Philologus* 100 (1956), p. 169; M. L. West, ed., *Hesiod: Theogony* (Oxford, 1966), p. 162; M. Griffth, "Personality in Hesiod," *Classical Antiquity* 2 (1983), p. 48, n. 46.

tion between different kinds of poetry, but rather a more specific contrast between those poets to whom the Muses tell the truth and those to whom they tell falsehoods.

The true difficulty with the standard view is that it imposes a reductive reading on the text by failing to take into account the unsettling threat in the Muses' words. The Muses can, according to their inclination, tell either truths or plausible falsehoods. The falsehoods are dangerously misleading since they have the ring of truth. Hesiod claims no power to evaluate the truth or falsity of the Muses' words, and he makes no suggestion that his intended human audience could have any such power. The sole source of Hesiod's poetry is the Muses' divine voice, which itself withholds any guarantee of it own truth. So, however faithfully the poet transmits from his source, he cannot promise his audience that the account of the gods they will hear is accurate, since no additional human resource can check the Muses' veracity. All its divine source ensures is that the poem will possess verisimilitude. To be sure, the Muses are said to supply Hesiod's power to speak of the past and future (32). In another context, this might naturally imply that he is given the power to speak of the *real* past and future, that is, an epistemic power to speak authoritatively and accurately. Here, however, Hesiod's is a gift from Muses who have just been characterized as capable of dissembling. Thus, the standard interpretation of these lines cannot be accepted: the poet's power to relate the Muses' messages cannot ensure that he conveys anything that is true.[10] It follows that those interpretations that see an implication that poetry—and Hesiod's *Theogony*—contains falsehood, are mistaken in a crucial respect: they assume incorrectly that the Muses state or imply something definitive about the subject matter of the *Theogony* (or any other poem for that matter), when in fact they do not. The Muses precisely do not give any indication of whether the poem is true or false; they dangle the possibility of falsehoods before an audience that is incapable of distinguishing the two.[11] The story of Hesiod's encounter with Muses, then, focuses not on characterizing the poem as true or false, but on human beings' lack of knowledge of whether it is true or false, that is, on the epistemological limitations of mortals.[12] Scholarly efforts that would explain modes in which the Muses de-

[10] Contra Griffith 1983, p. 49, then, Hesiod's "unique proof" of the Muses' favor (his receiving the laurel staff and divine voice, *Th.* 30–34) does not unambiguously settle the question of whether his poem contains truth only.

[11] See Walsh 1984, p. 33: "far from justifying Hesiod and themselves, they [the Muses] locate their art beyond public judgment, for they suggest that human audiences will never be able to distinguish or appreciate either their truthfulness or their deceptive skill."

[12] Contra Walsh 1984, p. 27, then, the Muses, unlike Odysseus, are not portrayed as "successful deceivers," but only as *capable* of successful deception. We cannot know whether or not we see the Muses as deceivers in action, whereas we do know when Odysseus engages in deceptive storytelling. And this brings out what is perhaps the crucial disanalogy between the

ceive, or elaborate special meanings of "falsehoods that seem real" are misplaced. These attempts violate Hesiod's portrayal of the Muses as wielding a *mysterious* power and as capable of employing that power to generate plausible falsehoods. The mystery excludes any human knowledge of the truth or falsehood of poetry that records the Muses' superhuman reports. The rhetorical power of the Muses' words relies on the inexplicability (from the human perspective) of their means of deception and the precise nature of their deceptions. For the interpreter, the crucial issue regarding the Muses' words is not how they might be compatible with Hesiod's guaranteeing his poetry's truth, but rather, how Hesiod can exploit the possibility that what the supernatural source of his poetry conveys is false.

A current, sophisticated line of interpretation applies to the Muses' words a contemporary theoretic apparatus and has done more justice to the philosophical subtlety of Hesiod's thought. Work by M. Arthur, G. Ferrari, and especially P. Pucci, uncovers the complexity of the *Theogony*'s proem and its connection to broader philosophical and conceptual issues.[13] These studies have nevertheless tended to read the Muses' words at 27–28 in accord with assumptions that, in my view, obscure their true import. Although Pucci and Ferrari disagree in their interpretation of the lines, both maintain that the Muses propound a doctrine about language. For Pucci the Muses' words imply the Derridean thesis that an inherent obliquity, indirectness, or deferral characterizes language, including the Muses'. Language can be an accurate or inaccurate representation—and this is precisely the distinction the Muses make—but in both cases it fails to be entirely transparent because language inevitably distorts the signified. Ferrari relatedly argues that the Muses propound a thesis about false language only. On his view, the Muses point to a linguistic asymmetry between truth and lies, which must be understood in the broader ethical context of a distinction between what he calls "good and bad exchange." Each interpretation holds that Hesiod's view of the Muses articulates a general thesis about language. I would suggest, however, that although the Muses do propound a thesis about language, it is a thesis about *using* language, a thesis boasting of their own *power to manipulate* language. The Muses claim to have the power to speak truthfully, or to tell falsehoods that appear true. The power to deceive in particular boasts a formidable command of the logos. The Muses' remarks, then, do not articulate a view about how the nature of language itself shapes the Muses' speech. Rather, they declare the Muses' facility with language, and their consequent power and willingness

Muses and Odysseus: the Muses are divine, and Odysseus is mortal. There is therefore no reason to think that the nature of the Muses' deception is intelligible to mortals. I can thus see no basis for Walsh's suggestion that like Odysseus's, the Muses' falsehoods are true in substance but not in detail.

[13] Pucci 1977; Arthur 1983; Ferrari 1988.

to deceive human beings. Their remarks also presuppose a privileged position from which they withhold from humans knowledge of what they report, whether truthfully or not.

Neither the poet nor his audience, then, knows whether the Muses speak truthfully. The Muses' threat of deception calls upon their power to manipulate language. The resulting skeptical predicament neither disappoints the audience's expectations, nor weakens the poet's stature. I suggest, rather, that Hesiod reports the Muses' remarks in order to exploit the audience's anxiety about the divine power to deceive. He thereby aligns his poetry with a formidable power, even as he effectively disowns responsibility for his poem's truth or falsity. The result exempts his poem from evaluation on grounds of accuracy. It is not the case, however, that Hesiod thereby openly acknowledges the fictionality of poetry.[14] Difficult to believe as it is that Hesiod and other poets did not to some degree recognize the element of fiction in their own poetry, it is quite another thing for them to introduce a conception of the fictional as an explicit component of their poetics. As with Homer, one cannot assume that Hesiod fashioned his poetics to reflect nothing but his actual understanding of poetry; surely poetic and rhetorical considerations enter into it and prompt the poet to formulate his poetics not as a transparent reflection of how he understands the nature of poetry, but rather, as a reflection of how he would like poetry to be viewed by the audience. A concept of fictionality would, in fact, conflict with the substance and purposes of Hesiod's skeptical poetics; such a concept would presume the literal falsehood of Hesiod's poetry, while the skepticism governing his poetics denies any such certainty. It is not, then, fictionality or artistic invention that Hesiod introduces, but rather the consequence that the divine power to deceive holds sway over human knowledge. These skeptical implications are undiminished by Hesiod's connection to the supernatural. On the contrary, Hesiod's theory submits the poet to the Muses' powers of deception. Still, if the Muses' power diminishes the poet, it fortifies his poetry. Hesiod credits the Muses with a formidable and mystifying power over human beings to which his theory subjects the audience of his poem. Because of its privileged connection to divinity, his poetry inherits the Muses' divine force as well as its characteristic perils.

Another motive for the Hesiodic theory of poetic deception emerges when we press certain issues surrounding the role of interpretation. Assigning a specific positive task to interpretation might be a natural response to the inherent uncertainty of poetry's truth. But Hesiod's theory debars interpretation from playing such a role, since it claims that it is impossible for mortals to discover poetry's truth-value. Apprehending that value

---

[14] As M. Heath suggests, "Hesiod's Didactic Poetry," *CQ* 35 (1985), pp. 258–59.

would require independent criteria established for interpretation, and those criteria would contribute to a philosophical approach to the interpretation of poetry. The question asked of poetry would be whether or not it says something true, not, for example, how it's imagery and language function or how it connects with a particular social or historical context. As we shall see, Socrates' interpretive approach to poetry brings to bear just such a philosophical orientation. But on the Hesiodic view, interpretation that seeks to establish poetry's truth proceeds in vain, since the power to know poetry's truth belongs among the exclusive privileges of the Muses. As Homer did with his theory of divine knowledge, then, Hesiod too aims to discourage a certain kind of interpretation from being applied to his poem. By exempting his poetry from dispensing divine knowledge, the poet attempts to forestall interpretations that would pass judgment on the truth or falsity of his poem. He thereby seeks to make himself, and his poem, invulnerable to criticisms that would assess the poem's truth, or seek to derive moral truths from its verses. Hesiod, it seems, wants his poem in this sense to remain uninterpreted, or rather, uninterpretable.

The Muses, then, are responsible for the truth or falsity of the poem—Hesiod has nothing to do with that, and he attributes neither to himself nor the audience the power to evaluate the poem in those terms. The contrast between the limitations of human knowledge and the Muses' superiority appears similar to the distinction between divine knowledge and mortal hearsay in *Iliad* 2. 484–87:

> Tell me now, Muses that have dwellings on Olympos—
> For you are goddesses, and are present, and know all things,
> Whereas we hear mere rumor and know not anything—
> Who were the captains of the Danaans and their lords?

Unlike Homer, however, Hesiod's theory does not imply that poetry traverses the usual boundaries between mortal and immortal. Hesiod's theory withholds from the poet and the audience access to divine knowledge. Hesiod turns away from issues of truth and falsity as beside the point of his poetry, irrelevant to his responsibility and power as a poet. This reading of the Muses' remarks makes sense of the tone of line 35, "but enough of this gossiping" (literally, "but what is my business round tree or rock"). Hesiod dismisses his initial invocation of the Muses as neither here nor there because it has focused on an aspect of poetry outside of the poet's domain, which bears on neither his talents nor his power over the audience. The proem begins again in line 36, where he turns to what concerns Hesiod and his audience more directly: poetry's practical function as therapy for the human psyche.

The poet has already hinted at the character of his own gift. The Muses, he says, have breathed into him a divine voice and given him a laurel staff, an emblem of his poetic gift. Hesiod receives the divine voice of the Muses, but the poetic power he thereby exerts is not necessarily divine. The laurel σκῆπτρον signifies a particular *human* power—that of the king—and the implied comparison between poet and king fashions one key element in what follows. The staff, moreover, as an object from the natural world, aptly represents a mundane talent, rather than a divine gift. Hesiod receives inspiration, and the *source* of his poetic gift is divine. These do not, however, require that the gift itself is a divine power. We have already seen that Hesiod is not endowed with the specifically divine capacity to know whether his poetry is true. The Muses breathe into Hesiod an αὐδὴν θέσπιν. As we shall see in the second half of the proem, there are further indications that the resulting poetic gift is not a divine power, although it *is* god-given.

Poetic Therapy as Mimesis

In the first part of the proem, then, the Muses grant Hesiod the power to sing, but they withhold something too: the power to discover whether poetry's content is true. The poet's and audience's capacities are thereby revealed as limited in comparison with the Muses'. In the second section, Hesiod also distinguishes the poet from the Muse. But there, rather than falling short of the Muses' intellectual capacities, the poet is shown to perform a practical function that the Muses do not perform.

Beginning at line 36 Hesiod vividly describes the Muses' singing on Mount Olympus in order to characterize, and influence, his own relationship to the audience. Through implicit comparison, the divine model of poetic experience flatters the mortal poet and audience. In their father's house, the Muses sing a theogony, and a song about mankind and the Giants. They induce pleasure and laughter in their divine audience; Zeus's household laughs as their voices fill the air (40), and Zeus in particular is said to delight in their song (37, 51). Hesiod too will sing a theogony, and through that parallel, he associates his own song with the object of divine pleasure, and his human audience with their divine counterparts. The mortal audience, then, sees itself, and the poet, represented on the divine plane. Hesiod offers his audience the outlines of an enhancing self-representation, and in that way begins already to relieve their troubled souls. In doing so, Hesiod performs the very function that he will self-consciously characterize when he states poetry's purpose.

Contrasts between the human and divine poetic theaters ensure the proper hierarchy and that the divine sphere is paradigmatic. The poetic performance on Mount Olympus appears to take place in an eternal present—the Muses are described as though they endlessly repeat the same performance[15]—the mortal version imitates, but falls short of, this eternal repetition and sameness. The human scene of poetic performance may in this way be said to reenact the primal, celestial institution. But although the dynamics of an oral tradition ensure that the elements of Hesiod's theogony have been, and will be, repeated, traditional poetry can only strive for a *long* life and can only approximate exact repetition. The divine scene of poetic performance serves as a prototype, then, and as such it dignifies, through comparison, its mortal imitation.[16]

Another discrepancy between the divine model and its human incarnation isolates the poet's particular gift to mankind. The Muses' singing, Hesiod emphasizes, delights Zeus and the other gods. This feature of their performance, that it typically causes pleasure, undoubtedly corresponds to Hesiod's view that the poet functions primarily as a therapist of troubled souls:

... ὅ δ᾽ ὄλβιος, ὅντινα Μοῦσαι
φίλωνται· γλυκερή οἱ ἀπὸ στόματος ῥέει αὐδή.
εἰ γάρ τις καὶ πένθος ἔχων νεοκηδέι θυμῷ
ἄζηται κραδίην ἀκαχήμενος, αὐτὰρ ἀοιδὸς
Μουσάων θεράπων κλεῖα προτέρων ἀνθρώπων
ὑμνήσει μάκαράς τε θεοὺς οἳ Ὄλυμπον ἔχουσιν,
αἶψ᾽ ὅ γε δυσφροσυνέων ἐπιλήθεται οὐδέ τι κηδέων
μέμνηται· ταχέως δὲ παρέτραπε δῶρα θεάων.

... Fortunate is the man whom the Muses
love: sweet words flow from his lips.
If someone has sorrow and is sick at heart
and stunned with fresh trouble on his mind, and a singer,
servant of the Muses sings of the glorious deeds of men in former
    times
or of the blessed gods whose home is Olympus,
he quickly forgets his bad thoughts and his cares
he no longer remembers: the gifts of these goddesses instantly divert
    the mind.

(96–103)

As the Muses' singing pleases the gods, so Hesiod's song will cause men to forget their cares. The similarity between the effects of the Muses' song

[15] ... τῶν δ᾽ ἀκάματος ῥέει αὐδὴ / ἐκ στομάτων ἡδεῖα· ("Sweet song pours from their mouths and never wearies" [39–40]).

[16] See Eliade's theory of reenactment of primal scene through myth and ritual (M. Eliade, *The Sacred and the Profane,* trans. W. R. Trask (San Diego, 1959), pp. 61–62).

and Hesiod's song fits with the pattern of comparison we have already noted; the occasion of poetic performance on earth mimics the celestial model. Their similarities make it easy to overlook an important difference. In the divine realm, the effect of song is simply pleasure. Zeus and the other gods are not presumed ill or in need of relief. In causing the gods pleasure, then, the Muses' singing does not aim to relieve a difficulty or divert a troubled mind. But just such therapeutic aims are the poet's. His human subjects are addressed as patients afflicted by psychic ills and in need of diversion. The human auditors differ from the divine audience; for the gods, poetry is merely a source of pleasure. For humans, poetry provides relief from workaday pain, and a respite from routine suffering. In both cases, poetry causes pleasure, but the aims of poetic experience in the two cases differ.

By comparing the poet to a king, Hesiod further defines and glorifies his role. Like the poet, the king's talents rely on a gift from the Muses. Kings, like poets, provide a kind of therapy to wounded parties, and they owe this power to a facility with language. Disputes are settled and just verdicts issued by the king's persuasive eloquence. His gentle words "flow like honey" (84) and win the eager consent of his subjects. The king is worshipped and revered like a god (91). The king's gift comes from the Muses, in particular from Calliope (80, 93). Although the king's power relies on a particular connection with Zeus (96), the Muses love both king and poet, and cause sweet words to flow from their lips (96–97). Hesiod has linked poetic with regal eloquence by tracing a common source in the Muses; the poet too, he implicitly suggests, is worthy of reverence. At this point (94) Hesiod ostensibly leaves the topic of kings and moves on to the poet exclusively, but in fact the comparison remains at work. As the king's gift allows him to settle disputes and political upsets, so the poet has the adjudicator's gift of relieving, at least temporarily, the *internal* strife and disharmonies of the soul. He does so through his poetry's tendency to induce forgetfulness. The comparison with the king works to extend poetry's benefits beyond those that Hesiod articulates explicitly. Presumably, the king actually ends disputes. But Hesiod's poetry, it may appear, merely treats the symptoms. Poetry diverts (παρατρέπω, 103) the mind, and so causes *temporary* forgetfulness. The royal analogy pushes poetry's function a step further to insinuate (without providing details) that it can aim to *cure* a soul of its troubles as the king aims to settle disputes.

The attentive reader will have noticed that the avowed therapeutic effect of Hesiodic poetry appears to be at odds with another rhetorical strategy we have seen at work in the proem. We saw how with the Muses' words at 27–28 Hesiod exploits the audience's anxiety about divine power as a way of enhancing the status and power of his own poem. This device for arousing anxiety seems to rest uneasily with the poet's view that his poetry provides soothing therapy for troubled souls. The tension, in fact, reveals something important about the nature of Hesiod's poetic therapy. Because Hesiodic poetics do not guarantee that poetry contains truth, it cannot be a reality-based therapy that poetry promises. Poetry cannot comfort and enchant by providing an unambiguously true account, but only through a pleasure-based therapy for which truth is irrelevant. The proem, then, aims first to elevate the audience's fear and uncertainty by invoking the divine power to deceive, and then, not to allay that anxiety, but perhaps to distract from it with a therapy of pleasing words. We will return later to further implications of this particular notion of poetic therapy.

We are now in a position to approach more broadly the question of how Hesiodic poetics envisions the purpose of the *Theogony*. This issue is often put in terms of didactic versus nondidactic intentions. Heath has argued that there is, at most, evidence that the poem is didactic in *genre,* which he distinguishes from its having a true didactic intent.[17] On Heath's reading of the poet's encounter with the Muses, Hesiod may (or may not) guarantee that his poetry conveys truth. If he does, then, according the Heath, the most we can say is that veracity is a *constraint* on the poem rather than a purpose. The *Theogony*'s central purpose, as elaborated in the rest of the proem, is to give pleasure and rest from cares.[18] A problem for this interpretation arises from its definition of didacticism. It assumes that poetry is didactic insofar as it aims to convey factual truth, and so it looks for evidence indicating that the poem guarantees its own veracity. But a more accurate definition would take didactic poetry to teach a lesson of some sort—often a moral lesson—and this does *not* necessarily depend on the poem's being factually true. Lessons of all sorts can emerge from false tales and fictional accounts. With that in mind, we can see that the question of the *Theogony*'s being didactic does not depend on its guaranteeing that its account of the gods is factually accurate in any detail. Still, the proem does not announce the forthcoming poem as didactic in any clear sense. Rather, the proem itself has a kind of didactic purpose. Hesiod's entire theory of poetry is didactic insofar as it articulates a theology and teaches the audience the (self-serving) lesson that they can emulate the gods by taking pleasure in the *Theogony*. By situating the audience in a mimetic relation to the gods, the poet in this respect defines the audience's relation to divinity. The danger of the Muses' deception also contributes to defining this relation, as mortals are seen as limited epistemologically and therefore at the mercy of the Muses' whims. Hesiod's aim in the proem is thus didactic insofar as it seeks to convey to the audience a particular account of their relation to divinity.

[17] Heath 1985, p. 259.

[18] Didactic and pleasure-giving purposes are not, of course, inherently incompatible—as we have seen with Homer. Their connection anticipates Aristotle's remark in the *Poetics* that mimesis is pleasurable.

The form of Hesiod's final invocation to the Muses raises important questions. As in Homeric invocations, the narrator's voice merges with the Muses', ambiguously suggesting that the poem's words issue directly from their divine source:

ταῦτά μοι ἔσπετε Μοῦσα Ὀλύμπια δώματ᾽ ἔχουσαι
ἐξ ἀρχῆς, καὶ εἴπαθ᾽ ὅτι πρῶτον γένετ᾽ αὐτῶν.
Ἤτοι μὲν πρώτιστα Χάος γένετ᾽ ·

Relate these things to me, Muses whose home is Olympus,
from the beginning; tell me which of them first came into being.
First of all, Chaos came into being . . .

(114–16)

Does the poet or the Muse speak line 116? Does this narrative structure imply that a divine power possesses Hesiod, that the audience experiences a divine voice directly? In Homer it did, but there, the narrator himself is habitually oblique, withholding a clear sense of himself as an embodied individual, and he is portrayed as a communicator of divine knowledge. Not so with Hesiod. Divine knowledge is inaccessible to him, along with other mortals, and as the proem develops his own personality, we have seen that it distinguishes the effects of his song from the effects of the Muses' song. Hesiod, for example, is a shepherd, chided by the Muses for stereotypical laziness. This characterization enforces a sense of the poet as a distinctly mortal being.

But perhaps the Muses' "breathing into him" a "divine voice" constitutes an announcement of divine possession. The view that poets wield a divine power appears compatible with, and even suggested by, aspects of Hesiod's poetics, including his account of the divine voice and the narrative structure of his final invocation. But other aspects of the text suggest a more distinctly human power at work: Hesiod first of all lacks divine knowledge of poetry's truth. The Muses grant him the power to sing of the past and future, but with that comes no guarantee that he sings truths rather than falsehoods and no resource for telling the difference between the two. Furthermore, as a distinctly mortal figure he performs a task—diverting human beings from their sorrows—that does not appear necessarily superhuman. In this case the Muses would endow the poet—and the king—with a special *human* power, rather than make him an instrument of divine power. Finally, although the striking similarities between Hesiod's theogony and the Muses' various songs provide the basis for a mimetic relationship, it has been shown that the Hesiodic and divine songs clearly diverge in content, perspective, and inclusiveness.[19] Hesiod's theogony, for example, unlike the Muses' song, does not include an account of the race

[19] Clay 1988.

of men and giants, and it organizes its material differently.[20] If Hesiod does not transmit the Muses' song, but creates a song of his own, then he does not serve as a mere vehicle for divine song. In this respect the Hesiodic poet differs dramatically from his Homeric counterpart who represents himself serving as transmitter and mouthpiece for the divine voice.

But the question of how Hesiod represents his connection to divine power is complicated by issues about the Hesiodic notion of inspiration. Consider first the Muses, and the power they wield. How does the text define their poetic power? As doyennes of the poetic art, how does Hesiod's presentation of them articulate *poetry's* power? When the nature of their power becomes clearer, then we can ask whether the poet receives that power in virtue of his connection to the Muses. The Muses' poetic influence appears to manifest itself in two separate powers, which are perhaps necessarily linked. The first of the Muses' powers appears as a privilege withheld from and lorded over human beings. As we have already seen, the Muses use this epistemological privilege as a dominating force: they know how to speak the truth and how to compose, at will, falsehoods that appear true. The Muses can, then, discriminate between truth and falsehood in poetry. They are tied directly to reality. That is, they have access to what is real as if through a window, and they can compare a poetic composition and successfully evaluate whether it represents that reality. Knowledge and evaluative capacity *withheld* invests the Muses with superiority and an aura of influence. In this context poetry's power appears to be pure authority, authority without enlightening communication. The Muses must be revered as wise and the ground of their wisdom acknowledged, but they do not demonstrate their knowledge, they do not share it with human beings. The Muses' second power differs considerably and manifests itself in a communicative function. In their performance of poetry, the Muses characteristically give pleasure to the gods. They can thus be said to possess and exercise the power to cause delight with their poetry, to charm their audience.

As we have seen, the poet disclaims the Muses' first power, their divine knowledge of poetry's truth. To that extent, it would seem that the poet does *not* exercise a divine power. If the Muses' only power were their particular sort of divine knowledge, then the poet's connection to the Muses would not invest him with the relevant divine power. But in the case of the Muses' second power, a direct transmission to the poet may appear to occur. The poet's therapeutic power over his audience mimics the Muses' power to please, and this mimicry might be said to dramatize the poet's direct connection to divinity. Given their relationship to the poet, it might follow naturally that the Muses endow him with their own power. The

[20] Clay 1988, pp. 325, 329.

poet's power to alleviate suffering would then be an exercise of the Muses' divine power. The Muses would act *through* the poet, with the poet serving merely as vehicle. The poet's performance would have a different effect, since it relieves the pain of a presumably afflicted audience. But it is nevertheless the Muses' song, and exercises only the Muses' power.

But a different reading of the poet's relation to the Muses is compatible with Hesiod's text, and fits more accurately the poet's self-representation. Unlike the Homeric narrator, Hesiod's gives a forceful sense of his ego and identity. The whole feeling of Hesiod's proem differs from Homer's invocations, and this general feeling is produced by a particular self-consciousness, a particular sense of the narrator's presence and of his being aware that he is sketching a representation of himself. For example, with his remark in line 35 that what he has said up to this point is "neither here nor there," the poet reflects with an offhand personal judgment on his own composition. The poet's ego hovers at the surface in his remarks regarding the great fortune bestowed upon the man whom the Muses love, and in his defining the poet's power and skill. The ostensible generality of these remarks has clear implications for Hesiod and descends to a kind of bragging. All in all, Hesiod gives us the sense that he is a *somebody* with individual characteristics and personality traits. This self-representation does not correspond to a view that would see the poet as a mere vehicle for the Muses' poetry, as a passivity and a blank slate. It coheres much better with a modified account of the poet's relation to the Muses. On this account the Muses endow the poet with a power of his own rather than making him a transmitter of their divine power. The poet is not possessed by the Muses, but granted a gift from them. This configuration implies that the poet does not wield, and therefore does not transmit to his audience, a divine power, but a human version of a divine power. The Muses breath into him a divine voice, but what comes out is the product of a *human* skill. In their experience of poetry, then, the audience is insulated from direct contact with the Muses' supernatural singing. To accommodate this interpretation, the narrative structure of the final invocation to the Muses, insofar as it implies that the *Theogony* issues directly from the Muses' voice, must be taken as a formality, not a literal suggestion that the Muse narrates the *Theogony*. It is not difficult to do so, given the poet's self-reflective presence throughout the proem, and the implication that promotes him above any mere transmitter of divine song.

Personality in Hesiod

In speaking of Hesiod as an individual personality and the implications this has for his conception of the poet, I have touched upon an important critical controversy that deserves discussion. The general contrast I have drawn between Hesiod's self-expression and Homer's obliqueness in certain respects follows the traditional *Geistesgeschichte* that sees Hesiod as the first self-conscious voice in European literature. This view has exerted a powerful force on Greek scholarship. But in fact neither the traditional account nor a recent attempt to challenge it has, in my view, captured precisely the shift we see taking place in the Hesiodic author. Moreover, as I will argue, the terms of this debate are in many ways inaccurate and confusing. It is not clear, for example, that "self-consciousness" best describes what Homer lacks and Hesiod introduces.

With its roots in Hegelian philosophy and Romantic literary theory, the traditional account places Hesiod in a broader history of Greek consciousness, as the first poet to express awareness of himself as a distinct personality and self. Whereas the Homeric narrator merges almost entirely with the traditions and conventions of his literary form, Hesiodic poetry, according to this view, inaugurates a new stage in the development of literary expression and in the expression of human spirit. The poet now includes autobiographical and personal elements in his writing, which expresses his own emotions and beliefs. This new sort of poetry calls for a different kind of evaluation: interpreting the literary conventions within which the author works must give way to the kind of interpretation typified by Romantic criticism, where the biographical study of the poet and a focus on his artistic imagination take precedence. This standard account has been used to explain an apparent shortcoming of Hesiodic poetry. What many have seen as a lack of design and illogical sequences of thought resulting from an unrefined, primitive mentality can instead be viewed as products of the author's spontaneous and unique artistic imagination.

This description of Hesiod's place in the developing self-consciousness of Greek literature and culture, which many scholars have accepted, was forcefully articulated in the influential works of Bruno Snell and Werner Jaeger.[21] But it has more recently come under attack. Taking his lead from work on lyric poetry (Pindar in particular) that has replaced biographical criticism with issues of genre, convention, and rhetorical stance,[22] Griffith argues that Hesiod's "autobiographical" voice should be viewed instead as a conventional persona shaped by artistic, not personal, purposes.[23] Moreover, Griffith presupposes that Homer and Hesiod work within similar conventions in concluding that the traditional view is mistaken to see any real innovation in the Hesiodic narrator.

[21] Snell 1953; Jaeger 1945; G. Misch, *A History of Autobiography in Antiquity*, vol. 1 (Reprint, Westport, 1973), pp. 73–75.

[22] E.g., E. L. Bundy, *Studia Pindarica*, 2 pts., *University of California Studies in Classical Philology* 18 (1962).

[23] Griffith 1983.

This type of analysis successfully counters the critic who reads the auto-biographical element in Hesiod as *gratuitous* self-expression. Surely we must admit that the Hesiodic narrator adopts poetic personae—that of "wisdom poet" in the *Works and Days,* and in the *Theogony,* a "grammar of self-reference" appropriate for hymnic and encomiastic poetry. The strongest evidence Griffith provides comes from the poems themselves. Of most immediate interest for our discussion is the proem to the *Theogony.* Here Griffith shows how Hesiod's description of the Muses enhances the poem by establishing Hesiod's relation to the Muses: by telling the story, Hesiod establishes his credentials as a poet specially empowered by the goddesses. Griffith goes on to suggest, more tentatively, that Hesiod's story of his encounter with the Muses might also serve to establish a certain relationship to his specific audience. His encounter with the Muses (and the subsequent comparison of poets to kings) provides grounds for kings to take this lowly shepherd seriously. The poet thus secures a position for himself as a legitimate authority among kings. By showing in these ways that the story of Hesiod's encounter with the Muses carries out a poetic agenda—what can be described, in general, as Hesiod's establishment of his authority as a poet—Griffith shows us how naïve it would be to suppose that Hesiod's only motive in describing his encounter with the Muses is self-expression: we cannot say for sure whether Hesiod's account is autobiographical, but we can see clearly the artistic and propagandistic purposes it serves.

The further point, that Hesiod's narrative persona in the *Theogony* is a conventional one essentially the same as Homer's, raises more difficulties. There is no doubt that Homer's reflections on the nature of poetry and the poet, particularly in the *Odyssey,* mark him as a self-conscious artist. But inferring that the only thing that distinguishes the Homeric from the Hesiodic narrator's self-expression is Homer's failure to mention his own name—and that only because he does not have a particular audience in mind—paints a misleading picture of continuity. As we have seen, the Homeric narrator is self-conscious in those key moments when the poem reflects on the nature of poetry and the poet. In supplying a theory of poetry and the poet, Homer appears, insofar as he is a poet, to imply something about himself. The "self" to which the Homeric narrator refers, however, may very well be a poetic persona. In that case, the narrator does not intend necessarily to disclose autobiographical information, but does adopt a particular persona for artistic reasons. For example, given the rhetorical purposes that I have argued are at work in the Homeric theory of poetry, it would stand to reason that in sketching his theory of the poet and poetic experience, Homer assumes a persona (that may or may not conform to his actual self). The point foremost in his thought is not accurate autobiography, but rather advancement of a view of poetry and the poet (and himself) that affects the audience by enriching their experience of his own poetry. It may be the case that in some ways he gives an accurate picture of himself, but only accidentally, since his purposes do not include accurate self-expression, but the expression of a persona that contributes to his artistic design. To the extent that both Homer and Hesiod reflect on the nature of poetry and thereby imply a theory of poetry and the poet, they share what we might assume are general conventions of "self"-expression.

Or so it seems. In fact, when we look more closely at the Homeric narrator's persona, the matter becomes more complicated. Homer expresses a "self," but this persona, as we have seen, characterizes the poet as a mere conduit for the Muse's voice, a cipher with only a passive function. The poet's role as craftsman (and Circe-figure) comes only as a component in the Homeric theory of poetry; it is not personified in the narrator. Homer's narrative persona thus aims to conceal the author in the very act of revealing him: the narrator depicts himself as having no personality as such and in this way forestalls inference about his personality. But anonymity is not the most accurate characterization of this narrative stance. The narrator represents himself as having a privileged and exceptional connection to the Muses, and this marks him out as far from anonymous. And yet, personality as such does not enter the picture. The narrator represents his ego as concealed by his purely passive function (whether it actually is concealed is another matter)—he is, on his own account, a mere vehicle. We can for these reasons say that the Homeric narrator adopts the authorial persona of a *conduit*. This obliqueness advances a view of poetry, and in this way serves poetic purposes.[24]

Hesiod's narrative persona in the proem to the *Theogony* contrasts sharply with the Homeric narrator's, and it is here that we can locate a major shift taking place. With parallels in Theognis and the *Homeric Hymn to Apollo*,[25] the Hesiodic narrator adopts a full-fledged autobiographical persona, by which I mean that he adopts the persona of an author giving autobiographical details, including evidence of his ego and personality. With Hesiod, the author's persona as narrator is moved onto the stage and becomes a character in his own poem. In naming himself and casting himself as an actor in the poem, Hesiod departs in important ways from the Homeric narrator. It is one thing for Homer to represent the bards Demodocus or Phemius; it would be quite another for a "Homer" to appear as a character in his own poem. Hesiod makes just this move, and with it engages in a sort of self-dramatization foreign to the Homeric narrator. Hesiod employs the narrative persona of *author as character* for specific artistic pur-

---

[24] *Pace* Griffith, the narrator's obliqueness is thus not only the result of Homer's addressing a generalized rather than local audience.

[25] *Homeric Hymn to Apollo* 165–78; Theognis 19–38. See Griffith 1983, pp. 42–47.

poses, and these go beyond his desire to establish his authority as a poet. After all, the Homeric narrator establishes his authority by *withholding* his personality and never speaking in the autobiographical mode—this stance allows him to project himself as the mouthpiece of the divine voice. What, then, does Hesiod gain by introducing an autobiographical persona?

As we have seen, the Hesiodic narrator uses the autobiographical mode to propound a particular view of poetry and the poet—a view that differs in significant ways from Homer's. For Hesiod, poetry's value is therapeutic, and the poet's gift mundane, whereas for Homer, poetry provides divine knowledge through a poet who wields a divine power. Hesiod adopts the autobiographical mode to make his theory more persuasive. His personable and all-too-human narrator is closer to the humans he attempts to divert than Homer's narrator is; since Hesiod's narrator has experienced human ills and presumably still suffers from them, he is in a better position to address the audience's ills. The autobiographical mode also helps Hesiod's theory persuade in a different way, by making it seem as though it is not a *theory* at all. With any poetic narrator there is an inherent ambiguity as to whether the persona he adopts does or does not reflect his true self. An assumption either way is unwarranted, and the ambiguity forms one of the poem's artistic elements. But when a narrator adopts the persona of author as character, that is, when he engages in the self-dramatization of the autobiographical mode, the ambiguity is particularly pronounced. When Hesiod assumes the persona of an author engaging in autobiography, then, we are especially inclined to assume that he is indeed revealing something true about himself, since he speaks so straightforwardly of "Hesiod's" encounter with the Muses. The assumption must be resisted, but, I would urge, the ambiguity—in particular the suggestion of literal autobiography—is something Hesiod exploits in the service of his theory of poetry. By articulating a poetics through an "autobiographical" episode, Hesiod encourages viewing the theory as though it is not a theory at all, but an autobiographical datum, invulnerable to the sort of evaluation that a theory invites. Hesiod presents his poetics, then, not as an attempt to persuade us of a theory that accounts for data, but as plain factual truth, a device that tends to lure the reader into accepting the theory uncritically.

For both Homer and Hesiod, then, self-expression is a narrative device. But the "self" expressed by Hesiod differs markedly from the one expressed by the Homeric narrator. This is where the interesting shift takes place in conventions of self-expression; the shift from Homer to Hesiod is one in the *mode* of self-expression, the nature of the narrative persona, not in the existence of self-expression or self-consciousness. While the Homeric narrator presents himself as a mere conduit for the Muse's voice, a pure passivity, Hesiod's narrator installs himself and his personality as a character in his own poem. Hesiod exploits the autobiographical mode, I have argued, for the rhetorical purposes of his theory of poetry.

We have seen that many distinguishing features of Hesiodic poetics are best revealed against the background of their Homeric counterparts. In Homer, the poet's virtue involves his transmission of divine knowledge to his audience. He does so by speaking as though he were actually present at the events he describes. He can speak as though he is present, with the privilege and authority of a divine perspective, because the Muses supply him with their divine perspective on epic events. For the Homeric Muses are present at the scene of epic events; they are knowers, apprehending those events, and they make the poet, and consequently the audience, into divine knowers too.

By contrast, the Hesiodic Muses are not described as present at the scene of epic events, though they are indeed stationed on the divine plane. Instead of apprehending epic events, they confine conduct of their performances of poetry to a divine audience in Zeus's house. These Muses, then, are divine *poets,* and their mundane counterparts are divinely endowed not with knowledge, but with curative skill. The Hesiodic poet's relation to the Muses differs accordingly from the relation that obtains between the Homeric bard and his Muse. Whereas the Homeric bard's Muse inspires by instilling divine knowledge in the poet, the Hesiodic poet's relation to his Muses is *mimetic.* Indeed, as we have seen, Hesiod juxtaposes the earthly scene of poetic performance to a divine model that it parallels. The poet's activity mirrors the Muses' in several ways. First, the poet's therapeutic skill enacts a human version of the Muses' power to please and delight their divine audience. Second, the poet mimics the Muses' tyrannical attitude to human beings. The Muses' divine knowledge of poetry's truth-value manifests itself as a tyrannical power lorded over mortals. The Muses are the despots of poetry who deceive at will and keep human beings in the dark in regard to whether poetry's content is true. The earthly audience is not promised the privilege of divine knowledge, but reminded by its inaccessibility that they are, ultimately, subjects of divine rule. The Hesiodic poet mimics the Muses' tyranny by also treating the audience as subjects. For the poet views the audience as *patients* in need of his curative power. He *treats* them with his poetry. The Homeric poet, by contrast, conceives of his task not as subjecting his audience to treatment, but as opening access to a divine perspective and to divine knowledge.

The Hesiodic and Homeric theories also differ considerably in their implications for the nature of poetic experience. Homeric supernaturalism holds that the audience acquires supernatural knowledge in their experience of poetry, through a direct encounter with the divine. Poetic experience, although pleasurable, is *cognitive* insofar as it imparts knowledge. Hesiodic poetics express a naturalist rather than a supernaturalist position, firmly separating human from divine. The Homeric account merges the two by sharing divine knowledge with poet and audience. In Hesiod the Muses do not grant the poet divine knowledge and they do not speak through the poet. Rather, they endow him with the power to sing with a curative effect on his mortal audience. His therapeutic gift is a human imitation of the Muses' divine power to delight their audience. The earthly audience's experience is *noncognitive,* for poetry does not impart knowledge, but contributes by soothing, diverting, and relieving pain. By contrast, the Homeric theory claims that poetry functions by engaging the intellect and imparting divine knowledge. The Hesiodic poet turns away from issues of knowledge in order to state the parameters of his own influence. His virtue as a poet, he claims, does not depend on his conveying knowledge, but just on the therapeutic effect of his song.

Another dimension of the proem's poetics employs an implicit rhetoric. I have argued that Hesiod's theory of poetry is noncognitive in that it does not hold, as the Homeric theory does, that poetry conveys knowledge to its audience. This failure to convey knowledge could naturally be viewed as a shortcoming. But in that case, why should Hesiod choose to attribute a deficiency to his own poetry? I have already answered that question in part by suggesting that Hesiod wishes to distinguish his own talents from the Muses'. An additional answer is available. The Homeric theory that poetry imparts knowledge itself enchants the audience by suggesting that poetry connects them to an object of divine knowledge. Hesiod's theory enchants in a different way, by *denying* that poetry conveys knowledge. The noncognitive aspect of the Hesiodic theory mystifies poetry in ways that makes it alluring to its audience. Hesiod's poetry, he claims, works like a drug to relieve temporarily the mortal condition. The audience, denied access to divine knowledge, is explicitly denied knowledge of how the drug works. Poetry is thus conceived of by Hesiod as a kind of medicine from the gods, a mysterious drug administered by the poet, but understood only by goddesses.

Hesiodic poetics accordingly embraces the view that poetry's value does not depend on its conveying truths, but only on its effect. Or, its effect is at least the indication of its value on which Hesiod's account focuses. The Homeric view stands in sharp contrast since it links poetry's value to its conveying knowledge, and therefore, truth. Hesiod's theory of poetry at the same time maintains the Homeric aim of deflecting interpretation, although it achieves this end differently. Hesiod's skepticism denies any role to interpretation that would seek to determine poetry's truth-value. Poetry's therapeutic effect, moreover, imposes no task of interpretation since poetry acts immediately on its audience with a curative effect. This view could even be said to immunize poetry against any efforts at interpretation, since it excludes attributing value to poetry beyond its immediate effect.

By means of skepticism and its claim to serve a therapeutic function, Hesiod's poetics attempts to deflect interpretation. We shall see that Pinder's theory of poetry innovatively introduces a role for interpretation as it posits the poet as the *interpreter* of the Muse's message. Yet Pindar's theory, although it admits the possibility of interpretation, attempts just as forcefully as Homer's and Hesiod's to preserve the poet's singular authority. By claiming the dogmatic authority of a *single* interpreter—the poet—Pindar's theory endeavors to suppress rival accounts as inferior to his own. A mixture of morality and politics, we shall see, lies at the basis of Pindar's dogmatism.

Chapter Three _____

Pindar: The Poet as Interpreter

LIKE HOMER and Hesiod, Pindar[1] petitions the Muse for a divine message:

μαντεύεο, Μοῖσα, προφατεύσω δ᾽ ἐγώ.

Muse, be my oracle, and I shall be your interpreter. (fr. 150)

Pindar, however, departs from both Homer's and Hesiod's poetics by casting the poet as an interpreter (προφήτης). Much of Pindar's poetic theory flows from this innovative model, including his radical conception of a poem as a decryption of a divine message from the Muse. Pindar's revisionary conception of the Muse as oracle also lends sense to his poetry's claim of authority: poetry interprets for its human audience a divine message that the poet receives as inspiration from the Muse.[2] Dodds took the narrator of this fragment to disavow all but an interpretive role: "observe that it is the Muse, and not the poet, who plays the part of the Pythia; the poet does not ask to be himself 'possessed,' but only to act as interpreter for the entranced Muse."[3] According to Dodds, the poet asks the Muse only for the "supernormal knowledge" required to grasp her message or act as her interpreter. But in fact the poet asks for more; he also asks that

---

[1] Ever since Bundy's rejection of the biographical approach to Pindar studies (see Bundy 1962) the groundwork has been laid for viewing Pindar's "I" as a poetic persona. Lefkowitz's defense of this position expounds the complex nature of Pindar's self-representation (Mary L. Lefkowitz, *First-Person Fictions: Pindar's Poetic "I"* [Oxford, 1991]; see especially "The Poet as Hero," pp. 111–26, and "The Poet as Athlete," pp. 161–68). Here I propose that the poet represents himself as a theoretician (on the nature of poetry) as well.

[2] Pindar's poetics are most often taken to be conventional elements of his poetry (see e.g., D. A. Russell, *Criticism in Antiquity* [Berkeley, 1981], p. 19; R. Hamilton, *Epinikion: General Form in the Odes of Pindar* [The Hague, 1974], pp. 113–15). This issue does not bear directly on the present study since I will be interested in showing how Pindar's poetics are bold and innovative only with respect to poetic theories outside the epinician tradition. It is nevertheless worth noting a weakness in the standard view: that Pindar touches on his poetics "briefly and allusively" (Russell, p. 19) need not imply that such topics were "expected and well understood." The brevity and allusive quality of these passages could instead simply result from their poetic, nondiscursive form.

[3] E. R. Dodds, *The Greeks and the Irrational* (Berkeley, 1951), p. 82, followed by Murray 1981, p. 97. Murray reads fr. 150 as claiming that the poet is an "intermediary between gods and men" in some general sense. The conclusion she draws from other passages, that for Pindar "poetic creativity depends both on inspiration and on conscious effort" is correct, but misses the particular nature of the poet's inspiration (reception of a cryptic message) and "conscious effort" (interpretation).

the Muse be his oracle. That must include a request, if not for ecstatic possession, then at least for inspiration that supplies him a divine message on which to exercise his interpretive skill.[4] Dodds's reading, then, misses the innovative division within Pindar's poetics that this fragment introduces: the distinction between the poet's reception of divine inspiration and his active production of poetry by transforming, through an exercise of interpretation, the divinely coded message into a poem. The poet is *both* inspired by the Muse's oracle and the interpreter of its divine message. Dodds correctly emphasizes that Pindar's invocation to the Muse requests no ecstatic state of divine possession. But unlike the publicly accessible messages of the Delphic oracle, the Muse communicates with Pindar's poet privately, by inspiration. Dodds is also correct in viewing Pindar's poet as gifted in "supernormal knowledge," for the poet's receptivity to divinely coded messages appears less like an ecstatic state than a cognitive one. Pindar's poet may be compared to a one-way bilingual translator who understands the language of the Muses and translates what he understands into the language of his human audience.

In portraying himself as an interpreter of the Muse's oracle, Pindar draws attention to himself as master of an ambiguous code that transmits some divinely certified truth.[5] But he does not mean to suggest, even in the most oblique way, that his interpretations constitute or "construct" a realm of truth.[6] That would imply an interpreter who does not discover truth, but fashions it himself through the persuasive power of poetic language. His use of oracle imagery to set forth his poetics goes out of its way to discourage any view that credits the poet with constructing the truths he communicates. It promotes instead the suggestion that he *discovers* them. Oracles utter coded messages of which interpretations are either cor-

---

[4] On the Muses communicating special wisdom to the poet, cf. also *Paean* 6. 50–53: "and as to whence the immortals' strife began, it is possible for the gods to entrust that to wise men, but mortals have no way to find it." *Paean* 7b. 15–23: "And I pray to Ouranos' well-robed daughter, Mnemosune, and to her children to provide facility, for blind are the minds of men, if anyone without the Helikonians seeks the deep path of wisdom."

[5] Pindar explicitly connects the Muse with Truth at *Olympian* 10. 1–6: Τὸν Ὀλυμπιο-νίκαν ἀνάγνωτέ μοι / Ἀρχεστράτου παῖδα, πόθι φρενός / ἐμᾶς γέγραπται· γλυκὺ γὰρ αὐτῷ μέλος ὀφείλων / ἐπιλέλαθ'· ὦ Μοῖσ', ἀλλὰ σὺ καὶ θυγάτηρ / Ἀλάθεια Διός, ὀρθᾷ χερί / ἐρύκε-τον ψευδέων / ἐνιπὰν ἀλιτόξενον. ("Read me the name of the Olympic victor, / the son of Archestratos, where it is written / in my mind, for I owe him a sweet song and have forgotten. O Muse, but you and Zeus' daughter, / Truth, with a correcting hand / ward off from me the charge of harming a guest friend / with false promises.") See also *Olympian* 4. 17–18; 6. 20–21; 7. 20–21; 13. 52; 10. 3–4; *Pythian* 1. 86–87; fr. 205; Murray 1981, p. 92; C. M. Bowra, *Pindar* (Oxford, 1964), pp. 26–33; Harriott 1969, pp. 69–70; Maehler 1963, pp. 96–98.

[6] Segal 1986, p. 143, speaks in this regard of Pindar's "self-consciousness of the construction of meaning in a poetry of 'truth' and 'presence'" and how in his model of oracle interpretation Pindar portrays himself as able to "constitute a realm of truth."

rect or incorrect; oracular utterances have a determinate meaning, a right
interpretation. In likening the poet to the specially skilled interpreter of an
oracle, then, Pindar claims that he is able to give the *correct* interpretation,
one that discovers (does not construct) its true meaning. To suppose that
Pindar's interpretations aim to provide merely a reading or a theory would
be to neglect his model of poetry as interpretation that captures a divinely
authoritative message.

A well-known passage from *Olympian* 2 echoes and begins to elaborate
the conceptions of fragment 150:

> . . . πολλά μοι ὑπ᾽
> ἀγκῶνος ὠκέα βέλη
> ἔνδον ἐντὶ φαρέτρας
> φωνάεντα συνετοῖσιν· ἐς δὲ τὸ πᾶν ἑρμανέων
> χατίζει. σοφὸς ὁ πολλὰ εἰδὼς φυᾷ·
> μαθόντες δὲ λάβροι
> παγγλωσσίᾳ κόρακες ὣς ἄκραντα γαρύετον
>
> Διὸς πρὸς ὄρνιχα θεῖον·

I have many swift arrows
under my arm
in their quiver
that speak to those who understand, but in general,[7]
they need
interpreters. The wise man[8] knows many things
by nature, whereas those who have learned [song], who
are boisterous
and long-winded, are like a pair of crows[9] that cry in vain
against the divine bird of Zeus.

> (*Olympian* 2. 83–88)

Pindar here contrasts the true poet with the apparent poet, and implicitly,
true poetry with apparent poetry. The true poet's arrows are missives from
the Muse coded in language the poet understands. Pindar may be taken to

---

[7] Alternatively, "for the whole subject," or "the crowd." W. H. Race, *Pindar,* vol. 1 (New
York, 1997), pp. 72–73 prefers the former and claims that the latter is unparalleled: "I interpret verse 83–88 to express Pindar's intention of dispensing with further details about the afterlife (as much as 'those who understand' might appreciate them), in order to provide a categorical evaluation of Theron's generosity." Race's reading has Pindar limiting the extent of
his subject matter—he will give a general, but not a detailed account of the afterlife. I read
the passage not as commenting on the preceding, but as a gnomic interlude and preface to
what follows.

[8] Pindar's "wise man" is self-referential.

[9] The crows may or may not refer to Bacchylides and Simonides. Cf. Race 1997, vol. 1,
p. 73.

suggest that his possession of "arrows" consists in his access to and unaided grasp of the meaning of the Muse's messages. The poet is clearer that his native skill distinguishes him from his competitors, whom he condemns as foolish and irreversibly ignorant enemies of legitimate poetry. Pindar relies on his claim to possess a naturally endowed wisdom to distinguish himself from his rivals. He declines to dispute whether the "long-winded pair of crows" are inspired, but he makes it clear that the true poet has both access to the Muse's oracular message and the poetic wisdom to understand and communicate its meaning. Since for Pindar natural talents constitute a divine blessing, Pindar's interpretive skill, his power of understanding, must also count as a gift that is god-given.[10]

By contrast, the merely apparent poet lacks natural knowledge. He relies upon "learning" rather than a natural cognitive resource to produce his poetry, which "cries in vain" for lack of any meaning.[11] It lacks meaning because either it is not inspired by the Muse, or, if it is inspired with an encrypted message from the Muse, the poet does not correctly interpret that message. This sort of poem is empty; it fails to drive at anything, although it may appear to. "Learning" has trained the apparent poet to compose poetry, but only such superficial poetry that merely sounds as though it is making a point, when its apparent poet lacks the "arrows" that would allow him to endow his efforts at poetry with meaning. Bad poetry is a boisterous cacophony, mere noise that lacks meaning. Pindar decries most poetry as bad poetry that burdens audiences with the interpretive task of making sense out of its mere noise. Strictly speaking, there is nothing in this bad poetry about which an interpretation could be right or wrong, since the poem itself lacks meaning. But interpreters are needed in order to *supply* and *invent* a meaning for the poem. This particular kind of interpretation is a specialized skill in itself. Meaning must be supplied from the outside, whereas any true poem contains its meaning intrinsically, as the poet's interpretation of his inspiration's divine significance. For the true poet's products, extrinsic interpretation is superfluous and bound to be inaccurate. Pindar's true poet does not produce poems that need an interpreter since he understands—and himself has interpreted—the divine message that his poem relates. Pindar thus attempts to forestall further interpretation of his poetry by a strategy different from either Homer's or Hesiod's. Homer did so by implying that his poetry provided audiences with quasi-perceptual di-

---

[10] Cf. *Pythian* 1. 41–42: "For from the gods come all means for human achievements, and men are born wise, or strong of hand and eloquent" (ἐκ θεῶν γὰρ μαχαναὶ πᾶσαι βροτέαις ἀρεταῖς, / καὶ σοφοὶ καὶ χερσὶ βιαταὶ περίγλωσσοί τ᾽ ἔφυν).

[11] Cf. the similar contrast between natural and learned abilities at *Olympian* 9. 100–104: "What comes by nature is altogether best. Many men strive to win fame with abilities that are taught (διδακταῖς), but when god takes no part, each deed is no worse for being left in silence."

vine knowledge. Hesiod told his audience that poetry acts on them as medication, with a therapeutic effect that is immediate. Pindar introduces a radically innovative theory of poetry, according to which a poem is itself an intrinsically meaningful interpretation of inspiration.

Pindar's praise poetry benefits from his innovative poetics. Unlike epic poetry, which allures and mystifies just because its subject matter is the Trojan war and the generation of gods in a legendary past, Pindar writes about protagonists in contemporary athletic events. The use of myth to connect the present with the legendary past is one of the techniques by which Pindar invests the present with universal weight. He also attempts to retain a certain mystification through his poetics. According to Pindar, the poet is not himself the source of his commentary on the contemporary events about which he writes. Rather, he interprets a *god's response* to those events: the victors provide the Muses with "work for their plow."[12] It falls to Pindar's poet to interpret and communicate the divine assessment. This configuration allows Pindar to assert his indispensable and active role in the composition of poetry. It also claims divine authority for the praise that his poetry distributes.

By casting himself in the role of interpreter, Pindar portrays the poet as playing an active role in the composition of poetry. But because the composition of poetry is defined by Pindar's theory as the correct interpretation of the Muse's message, the poet is not portrayed as creating new material. Thus, the suggestion that Pindar's use of εὑρίσκω at *Olympian* 3. 4–6 proclaims his active role in the *creation* of poetry cannot be correct.[13] There, Pindar relates that:

. . . Μοῖσα δ᾽ οὕτω ποι παρέστα μοι νεοσίγαλον εὑρόντι τρόπον
Δωρίῳ φωνὰν ἐναρμόξαι πεδίλῳ
ἀγλαόκωμον·

the Muse stood beside me as I found a newly shining way
to join to Dorian measure a voice
of splendid celebration, . . .

Taken on its own, this passage provides only ambiguous evidence: does the poet "find" what the Muse gives him or something of his own creation? We can decide by looking to Pindar's poetics. Pindar's claim elsewhere to be the Muse's interpreter suggests that what the poet here "finds" is his interpretation of a divine message supplied by the Muse. He thus portrays his effort in "creating" his poem as his attempt to provide the correct interpretation of the Muse's divine communication. In calling himself the Muse's interpreter, Pindar disdains any merely human evalua-

---

[12] Μοίσαισί τ᾽ ἔδωκ᾽ ἀρόσαι (*Nemean* 10. 26).
[13] Murray 1981, p. 97.

tion of his poem's subject in order to maintain his role as the Muse's own exegete.

Pindar's poetics are further elaborated at *Isthmian* 8. 56a–62, where the narrator enlists the Muses to praise the victor's deceased cousin Nikokles:

τὸν μὲν οὐδὲ θανόντ᾽ ἀοιδαί γ᾽ ἔλιπον,
ἀλλά οἱ παρά τε πυρὰν τάφον θ᾽ Ἑλικώνιαι παρθένοι
στάν, ἐπὶ θρῆνόν τε πολύφαμον ἔχεαν.
ἔδοξ᾽ ἦρα καὶ ἀθανάτοις,
ἐσλόν γε φῶτα καὶ φθίμενον ὕμνοις θεᾶν διδόμεν.

τὸ καὶ νῦν φέρει λόγον, ἔσσυταί τε Μοισαῖον ἅρμα Νικοκλέος
μνᾶμα πυγμάχου κελαδῆσαι. γεραίρετέ νιν, . . .

Not even when he [Achilles] died did songs abandon him,
but the Helikonian maidens stood beside his pyre and his tomb
and poured over him their dirge of many voices.
Indeed, the immortals too thought it best
to entrust a brave man like that, even though dead, to the hymns
   of the goddesses.

That principle holds true now as well, and the Muses' chariot is
   speeding forward
to sing a memorial to the boxer Nikokles. Praise him, . . .

Because of his great bravery, Achilles was judged deserving of the Muses' hymns even after his death. So too now, the Muses judge Nikokles worthy of praise on the basis of his bravery in the battles of the Persian war. They are "speeding forth" on their chariot and about to praise their subject. With the plural imperative, γεραίρετε, the poet signals the Muses to begin their song of praise.[14] With this invocation, the poet makes clear that the *Muses* praise their subject in both the present circumstances and in the mythical past to which he refers. The praise Pindar's poem offers is not merely analogous to or an imitation of the Muses' singing, but is in fact another instance of that singing. A divine "principle" (λόγον) determines the necessity for such singing: virtuous action is not only deserving of, but *necessitates* praise. Just as it was obligatory for the Muses to praise Achilles via song for his bravery, so too Nikokles will of necessity be praised by the Muses. The same principle that served as the basis for the Muses' hymning Achilles will serve as the basis of their song in praise of Nikokles. The poem's praise of Nikokles is thus conceived of as an automatic, because necessary, divine response to Nikokles' virtue. Insofar as it distributes praise according to the moral value placed on its subject, this divine response sets for humans a

[14] See Race 1997, vol. 2, p. 213, n. 4. The plural imperative is also addressed to the celebrants.

moral standard. And for the divine Muses, its performance is necessary just because it is morally required or obligatory.

Pindar here speaks as though his poem is being sung by the Muses. But his avowed role as their interpreter makes it clear that, unlike Homer's narrator, his own role is not as a divine transmitter. By attributing the ensuing praise to the Muses, then, Pindar must sustain the poet's active contribution as interpreter of the Muses' inspiration. This passage explicitly denies that the poet should be credited with *issuing* the moral evaluation that constitutes his poem's praise. Here we see that what the Muse's inspiration conveys is the *gods'* moral evaluation. The poet's composition must be understood, then, not to set forth judgments issuing from the poet himself, but to convey, as poetry accessible to all humans, divine evaluations which the poet dutifully endorses.[15]

A hint of this idea was already implicit in Pindar's conceiving of the Muse as his "oracle" and himself as a προφήτης. Oracles express the will of the gods. One who acts as a προφήτης of oracles expounds divine will. To say that he interprets is thus to say that, in his poetry, Pindar communicates the will of the gods. *Nemean* 9. 53–55 implies the same point when the poet prays that he surpasses other poets in casting his javelin nearest to the mark of the Muses.[16] To hit the mark of the Muses is to expound correctly divine will, and so Pindar characterizes his project in general as disclosing divine volition through an act of interpretation. The Muse's perspective on the human events with which Pindar's poetry concerns itself, then, is one that not only describes those events, but also expresses divine will with regard to them. We have seen how this more general conception of divine will is specified as the act of praise based on a principle of moral evaluation.

Poetry, Truth, and Deception

The truths that Pindar's poet claims he learns from the Muse and conveys authoritatively in poetry are the evaluations in his poems of praise. But as

[15] Walsh 1984, p. 42, claims that where Homer's poetics take all famous deeds to be suited to song, Pindar discriminates between those that are praiseworthy and those that are not: "Pindar's task is different from Homer's, and so he makes distinctions where Homer does not. Because Pindar praises or blames (and does not merely commemorate), he apportions the facts into two categories." But Walsh's formulation does not make it clear that, according to Pindar's poetics, the evaluation issues from the gods, not from Pindar himself. Pindar's *poetry*—insofar as it is the expression of divine judgment—not Pindar himself, selects and evaluates its material.

[16] 'O father Zeus, I pray that I may sound the praises of this deed of prowess by the favour of the Graces, and that I may excel many a bard in honouring victory by my verses, shooting my dart of song nearest of all to the mark of the Muses." (Ζεῦ πάτερ, / εὔχομαι ταύταν ἀρετὰν κελαδῆσαι σὺν Χαρίτεσσιν, ὑπὲρ πολλῶν τε τιμαλφεῖν λόγοις / νίκαν, ἀκοντίζων σκοποῖ᾽ ἄγχιστα Μοισᾶν.)

we shall see, Pindar also admits, and even draws attention to, poetic language's power to deceive.[17] Does acknowledging the possibility of deception in poetic language suggest that Pindar has a nascent conception of poetic fiction, an awareness that the "truth" poetry offers extends just to whatever it can persuade an audience to believe? If so, then Pindar's poetics would indeed illustrate a tension between a "poetics of presence" and a "poetics of textuality."[18] By examining the roles that truth and deception play in two passages crucial to Pindar's poetics, I shall argue that Pindar decidedly lacks any notion of poetic fiction and that his poetics, including his claim that poetry can deceive, relies on just the opposite: a simple conception of poetic truth as historical accuracy.

By appealing to moral criteria, Pindar's revision of the Tantalus myth in *Olympian* 1 attempts to persuade the audience of its truth. The standard legend that Pelops fed his son to the gods is "beyond the true account" (ὑπὲρ τὸν ἀλαθῆ λόγον, 28b) and "deceives by means of elaborate lies" (ψεύδεσι ποικίλοις ἐξαπατῶντι, 29). Pindar concludes that the standard account is false by arguing from its immorality: "It is proper for a man to speak well of the gods, for less is the blame" (35), and again, "But I for my part cannot call any of the blessed gods a cannibal—I stand back" (52). Pindar thus appears to argue that the standard version can be rejected on the ground that it attributes immoral behavior to the gods.

On the bases of such passages, the case has been made for understanding epinician "truth" as a specialized sort. What is epinicianly true is what is appropriate, and what is epinicianly false is what is inappropriate.[19] In epinician poetry appropriateness usually manifests itself as the correct apportionment of praise, and inappropriateness as the improper attribution of blame. According to this line of thought, the standard Tantalus myth is "false" only in the sense that it is inappropriate. It attributes reprehensible behavior to the gods to whom attribution of such behavior is inappropriate. On this view, then, Pindar does not necessarily claim that the standard myth misrepresents the gods, or that his version is more accurate. For "truth" and "falsehood" here refer only to a standard of propriety or moral value. It has even been argued that in this passage Pindar implies that praise poets like himself fictionalize, that he constructs a version of the Tantalus myth aiming not at factual accuracy, but at propriety, knowing full well, and even implying, that he is constructing a fiction.[20]

But this conflation of falsehood with impropriety reveals its incoherence upon closer examination of Pindar's text. Pindar contends that he

---

[17] The topic of much recent criticism. See, e.g., Feeney 1991, pp. 16–19 and bibliography provided there; Pratt 1993, pp. 115–29. On deception in ancient literature in general see C. Gill and T. P. Wiseman, eds., *Lies and Fiction in the Ancient World* (Austin, 1993).

[18] C. Segal, *Pindar's Mythmaking: The Fourth Pythian Ode* (Princeton, 1986), p. 31.

[19] Pratt 1993, pp. 115–29.

[20] Pratt 1993, pp. 123–26.

will not call the gods cannibals since it is improper to speak ill of them, and in fact dangerous, since it often leads to severe retribution, such as the speaker's impoverishment. If he were implying that his account of the Tantalus story were, or could be, fictional, and thus that the gods might very well be cannibals, then he would in effect be speaking ill of the gods and blatantly violating his expressed principle of propriety. It is thus unreasonable to suppose that Pindar jettisons the idea of factual truth in favor of defining truth strictly in terms of appropriateness. In order to apply coherently his own principle of propriety, Pindar must be claiming that the standard version of the Tantalus myth is factually false, and that his account is accurate or factually true. An assumption that would allow Pindar to argue from the moral impropriety to the falsehood of the standard myth is that the gods cannot engage in morally reprehensible behavior. Then he could reason that, if the gods are depicted as behaving so, then they are being depicted inaccurately. The result would include Pindar in the tradition of Xenophanes and Plato, who, as we have already mentioned, protest that the traditional myths are inaccurate on the ground that they attribute to the gods morally derelict behavior.[21] Pindar undoubtedly focuses on the moral dimension of the myth, but that is because for him too its moral content is indicative of, or grounds for inferring, its accuracy or inaccuracy. This passage, then, far from conflating moral truth with truth as accuracy, shows Pindar employing moral standards to judge factual accuracy. Those standards measure factual accuracy because Pindar is speaking of the gods: in the divine realm what is morally appropriate coincides with what is true. It has been argued that Pindar's revisions of the Tantalus story are motivated primarily by rhetorical needs rather than by religious scruples.[22] Indeed, the extent to which Pindar the man had personal religious scruples is impossible to infer from his poetry. But the *persona* he adopts for poetic purposes is of a man with religious scruples, and that is the crucial point. It is part of the author's rhetoric to adopt the stance of one who revises the myth in the light of moral standards. In this way it is impossible to separate the narrator's rhetorical purposes from his morality.

In correcting his poetic predecessors, Pindar often stresses the accuracy of his account:

> . . . ἐγὼ δὲ πλέον' ἔλπομαι
> λόγον Ὀδυσσέος ἢ πάθαν
> διὰ τὸν ἁδυεπῆ γενέσθ' Ὅμηρον·

---

[21] See Xenophanes DK 22 B 11; Plato *Republic* 377e–383c. Constrast Hesiod, whose imputations of immoral divine behavior are tempered by his poetics, which provide for the possibility that the Muse's song is false.

[22] A. Köhnken, *Die Funktion des Mythos bei Pindar* (Berlin, 1976), pp. 203–4, 206.

ἐπεὶ ψεύδεσί οἱ ποτανᾷ [τε] μαχανᾷ
σεμνὸν ἔπεστί τι· σοφία
    δὲ κλέπτει παράγοισα μύθοις. τυφλὸν δ᾽ ἔχει
ἦτορ ὅμιλος ἀνδρῶν ὁ πλεῖστος. εἰ γὰρ ἦν
ἓ τὰν ἀλάθειαν ἰδέμεν, οὔ κεν ὅπλων χολωθεὶς
ὁ καρτερὸς Αἴας ἔπαξε διὰ φρενῶν
λευρὸν ξίφος· ὃν κράτιστον Ἀχιλέος ἄτερ μάχᾳ . . .

        . . . I believe that Odysseus' story
has become greater than his actual suffering because
    of Homer's sweet verse,
for upon his falsehoods and soaring craft
rests a solemn spell, and his skill deceives
with misleading tales. The great majority
of men have a blind heart, for if they could have seen
the truth, mighty Aias, in anger over the arms,
would not have planted in his chest
the smooth sword. Except for Achilles, in battle he was the best . . .
                                            (*Nemean* 7. 20–27)

In this polemical posturing against his majestic predecessor, Pindar seeks
to assure his audience that he is divinely inspired. He draws attention to
the power of poetic language. A highly skilled poet like Homer can make
anything seem plausible, even what bears little relation to the truth. Although it can be used for deception, the mesmerizing power of poetic language is impressive and enchants the audience with the idea of poetry's
nearly magical qualities. Pindar thus evokes the enchantment of poetry in
general. In judging Homer's account inaccurate, Pindar implies that he enjoys the privileged knowledge necessary to have an opinion about whether
a poetic account of events is accurate or not. He thereby reasserts his claim
to command more than ordinary resources.

His next remarks, about Ajax, provide striking evidence that Pindar's
poetics lack a conception of poetic fiction. Having first warned his audience that they have been deceived by Homer because their reverence for
him has made them susceptible to his falsehoods, Pindar goes on to give a
surprising example. Most men are prone to deception and blind to the
truth, just as those were who, according to Pindar, wrongly judged Ajax
inferior to Odysseus. Had they seen that Ajax was indeed the superior one,
he would not have been driven to suicide. Pindar treats the men he claims
misjudged Ajax as *historical*, not fictional, figures, who demonstrate how
the run of mankind easily falls prey to falsehood. If they were merely the
fictional constructs of a poet, then Pindar could not cite them to demonstrate that point, but only that men are *depicted in poetry* as easily falling
prey to falsehood.

We are now in a position to draw some conclusions about Pindar's place in the development of early Greek conceptions of literary fiction. Recent criticism emphasizes Pindar's role in a developing awareness of poetic language's persuasive power. Truth is not a matter that pits fact over fiction, but solely a matter of what poetry has the power to make appear convincing through its particular charm.[23] According to this account, Hesiodic poetics began to question the Homeric assumption of poetry's truth by admitting the possibility that the Muses can fashion "lies similar to true things." Pindar pushes things a step closer to Simonides' more blatant claim that "appearance forces even truth."[24] Simonides' remark implies that there is no such thing as truth, but merely appearance; telling the "truth" is simply a matter of saying something persuasive.[25] Pindar is thought to move toward the Simonidean perspective by recognizing the "authenticating power of poetic language" in his own poetry.[26] The power of language to create the appearance of truth is, according to this view, displayed not only by the poetry Pindar criticizes as "deceptive," but, together with a certain amount of self-consciousness, by his own poetry. In his highly self-conscious revision of the Tantalus story, for example, Pindar describes the deceitful versions as "embellished" and "intricate."[27] But elsewhere he applies the same terms to his own poetry with no negative connotation.[28] Pindar's use of *Charis* to characterize song appears to be similarly double-edged. *Charis*, the poet claims, adds charm and authority *both* to the deceitful versions of the myth and to his own poetry.[29] Using examples like these as evidence, scholars have concluded that to some extent Pindar recognizes that "truth" "has its roots in the weird authenticating power of the poet's language."[30] In other words, truth depends on nothing more than what the poet can make appear convincing.

This account of the development of conceptions of truth confuses several issues and must be adjusted. Hesiod's poetics retains the idea of factual truth and holds to assumptions inconsistent with Simonides' radical

---

[23] G. F. Gianotti, *Per una poetica pindarica* (Torino, 1975), p. 62; Segal 1986; Feeney 1991, pp. 16–19.

[24] τὸ δοκεῖν καὶ τὰν ἀλάθειαν βιᾶται (fr. 598, *Poetae Melici Graeci*).

[25] Alternatively, we could take Simonides not to be making a general metaphysical claim, but rather celebrating (his) poetry's power to overcome previous beliefs about its subject matter; traditional views can yield to what his poetry says is true.

[26] Feeney 1991, p. 16.

[27] *Olympian* 1. 29: δεδαιδαλμένοι ψεύδεσι ποικίλοις.

[28] *Nemean* 8. 15; fr. 94b; See D. C. Young, "Pindar, Aristotle, and Homer: A Study in Ancient Criticism," *Classical Antiquity* 2 (1983), pp. 168–69.

[29] See J. Duchemin, *Pindare poète et prophète* (Paris, 1955), pp. 54–94; G. Kirkwood, *Selections From Pindar* (Chico, 1982), p. 52; on Charis and the Charites in general, see W. J. Verdenius, *Commentaries on Pindar*, vol. 1, *Mnemosyne* suppl. 97 (1987), pp. 103–106.

[30] Feeney 1991, p. 19.

view. In adopting his doctrine of the possibility that the Muses deceive, Hesiod assumes that there is some reality about which the Muses are either truthful or deceptive. For the Muses to exercise their powers to deceive by conveying falsehoods, there must be some truths about which they can deceive mortals. Hesiod does not, then, question the idea of factual truth. Unlike Homer, however, he does deny that poetry provides men with knowledge of that truth. Hesiod's innovation is epistemological rather than metaphysical: the audience is no longer provided a knower's master of any truths that Hesiod's poetry may convey. That there are truths to be shared or deceived about remains beyond question for Hesiod. In contrast, Simonides' view leaves no room for Hesiod's deception because for him there is no falsehood of which an audience can be persuaded.

Like Hesiod's, Pindar's poetics assumes that there are facts for poetry to convey. We have seen how, in his version of the Tantalus myth, Pindar promises to provide factual accuracy. Furthermore, in claiming that other versions of the tale are deceptive,[31] he shares Hesiod's assumption that there is something about which to be truthful or deceptive. Pindar renders human access to truth problematic, but in a way very much milder than Hesiod. Pindar's Muse is not a potential deceiver like Hesiod's; in this respect Hesiod's is the more radical, and Pindar's the more traditional, view. But as the interpreter of the Muse's "oracle," Pindar admits the possibility that the poet may misinterpret the Muse. For example, in fragment 205 he prays to avoid stumbling into falsehood.[32] For Pindar, then, human shortcomings rather than divine deception can break the audience's epistemological connection to the truth that poetry can convey. Although he admits the possibility of conveying falsehood, the focus in Pindar is on his poetry's truth.[33] It is not the authenticating power of poetic language that lies at the root of that truth, although Pindar indeed advertises the nearly magical power of poetic language and suggests that the particular charm of that language contributes to the persuasiveness of his poetry.[34] But the *truth* his poetry conveys holds independently of charm or persuasion. As we have

[31] ἐξαπατῶντι, *Olympian* 1. 29. See also *Nemean* 8. 32–35 where Pindar opposes πάρφασις (deception, allurement, misrepresentation) to his poetry in general: ἐχθρὰ δ᾽ ἄρα πάρφασις ἦν καὶ πάλαι, / αἱμύλων μύθων ὁμόφοιτος, δολοφραδής, κακοποιὸν ὄνειδος· / ἃ τὸ μὲν λαμπρὸν βιᾶται, τῶν δ᾽ ἀφάντων κῦδος ἀντείνει σαθρόν. / εἴη μή ποτέ μοι τοιοῦτον ἦθος ("Yes, hateful deception existed even long ago, / the companion of flattering tales, guileful contriver, evil-working disgrace, / which represses what is illustrious, but holds up for obscure men a glory that is rotten. / May I never have such a disposition).

[32] Ἀρχὰ μεγάλας ἀρετᾶς, / ὤνασσ᾽ Ἀλάθεια, μὴ πταίσῃς ἐμάν / σύνθεσιν τραχεῖ ποτὶ ψεύδει. ("Starting point for great achievement, Queen Truth, do not make my understanding stumble against rough falsehood.")

[33] Whereas Hesiod more radically detaches himself from such claims.

[34] See N. J. Richardson, "Pindar and Later Literary Criticism in Antiquity," *Papers of the Liverpool Latin Seminar* 5 (1985), p. 386.

seen, the truths that are particularly of interest to Pindar praise his subjects. The Muse reveals such truths to him in a cryptic form that the poet must interpret. If Pindar interprets the Muse correctly and conveys such truths to his audience, then he conveys the moral reality behind the gods' evaluation of the victory, the victor, and his kinsmen. Provided that Pindar's poems interpret their inspiration accurately, they convey the god's evaluation, not the poet's or not only the poet's. From a Socratic perspective, Pindar's poetics command no authority. Pindar will be vulnerable to the charge of promoting moral authoritarianism, adhering to moral evaluations grounded only in avowed divine authority. Socrates will expose the poet's claim to enjoy a natural, god-given knowledge as more often than not efforts to allow Pindar and others to uphold conventional, aristocratic values without defending them on any grounds more substantial than an appeal to divine decree.

Poetry and Its Effect

Pindar's distinctive portrayal of the purpose and effect of his poetry melds elements familiar from Homeric and Hesiodic poetics. For Homer, poetry conveys quasi-perceptual knowledge. For Hesiod it offers a pleasurable diversion and forgetfulness. Pindar's song offers a therapeutic relief from anxiety, as does Hesiod's. Pindar's prescribed treatment, however, is not forgetfulness, but knowledge.[35]

The beginning of *Pythian* 1 reflects on the nature of poetry, as Pinder invokes the Golden Lyre:

καὶ τὸν αἰχματὰν κεραυνὸν σβεννύεις
αἰενάου πυρός. εὕδε δ᾽ ἀνὰ σκάπτῳ Διὸς αἰετός, ὠκεῖαν πτέρυγ᾽
    ἀμφοτέρωθεν χαλάξαις,
ἀρχὸς οἰωνῶν, κελαινῶπιν δ᾽ ἐπί οἱ νεφέλαν
ἀγκύλῳ κρατί, γλεφάρων ἀδὺ κλάιθρον, κατέχευας· ὁ δὲ κνώσσων
ὑγρὸν νῶτον αἰωρεῖ, τεαῖς
ῥιπαῖσι κατασχόμενος. καὶ γὰρ βιατὰς Ἄρης, τραχεῖαν ἄνευθε λιπών
ἐγχέων ἀκμάν, ἰαίνει καρδίαν
κώματι, κῆλα δὲ καὶ δαιμόνων θέλγει φρένας ἀμφί τε Λατοίδα σοφίᾳ
    βαθυκόλπων τε Μοισᾶν.
ὅσσα δὲ μὴ πεφίληκε Ζεύς, ἀτύζονται βοάν
Πιερίδων ἀίοντα . . .

---

[35] As we shall see, contra Walsh 1986, forgetfulness has no place in Pindar's poetics. When Pindar at *Pythian* 1. 46 wishes the victor forgetfulness (ἐπίλασιν) from hardships, he is not invoking the emotional effects of poetry, but the consequences of having been praised: since the victor is now held in good repute, Pindar can hope that he will be free of hardship.

You quench even the warring thunderbolt
of ever-flowing fire; and the eagle sleeps on the scepter of Zeus,
   having relaxed his swift wings on either side,
the king of birds, for you have poured
over his curved head a black-hooded cloud, sweet seal for his eyelids.
   And as he slumbers,
he ripples his supple back, held in check
by your volley of notes. For even powerful Ares puts aside
his sharp-pointed spears and delights his heart
in sleep; and your shafts enchant the minds of the deities as well,
   through the skill of Leto's son and of the deep-breasted Muses.
But those creatures for whom Zeus has no love are terrified
when they hear the song of the Pierians . . .

(Pythian 1. 5–14)

Pindar here sounds the theme, recurrent throughout his poetry, of the soothing power of song.[36] As it "enchants" (θέλγει) their minds (φρένας), the lyre brings to Zeus's eagle and to the gods sleep, repose, and stillness.[37] Pindar employs a rhetorical strategy easily mistaken for Hesiod's appeal to a divine audience. Hesiod invites his audience to imitate the divine audience at a parallel scene of divine poetic performance in which the Muses' song delights the gods. The poet's performance, Hesiod urges us to believe, mimics the Muses'. The Hesiodic poet thus prompts his audience to imitate their divine counterparts and promises them an experience like Zeus's divine pleasure. Pindar also employs divine response to his poetry, but as the poet's performance of Pindar's ode begins, dwellers in the divine realm themselves respond to the *current* performance of Pindar's ode. Pindar includes within his own audience the gods, Zeus's eagle, as well as those whom Zeus despises. By extending his portrayed audience so that the gods listen and react to the very song that the human audience hears, Pindar imposes a standard for human responses to his poem, as it elevates its human auditors.

Pindar commends poetry generally for bringing to some a pleasurable relief from anxiety. To others, like the monster Typhos,[38] whom Zeus despises, it brings terror. The effect that song has on the enemies of Zeus gives us an important hint about the relief and rest that song confers on others. Why should those hated by Zeus be terrified when they hear the Muses' song? Their fear, I suggest, is caused by the fact that that song ex-

---

[36] Cf. *Olympian* 1. 30: Χάρις fashions all pleasant things (τὰ μείλιχα); *Olympian* 2. 13: the gods are soothed (ἰανθεὶς) by songs; *Nemean* 4. 3: songs soothe (θέλξαν) the victor; *Nemean* 8. 49–50: the charm of song (ἐπαοιδαῖς) can make "hard toil painless."

[37] See also *Olympian* 7. 7–8: poetry is "liquid nectar" and "sweet fruit of the mind" (φρενός).

[38] See *Pythian* 1. 15–28.

presses Zeus's judgment, and thereby evokes his great power. His disapproval directs fearsome power against them, so a reminder of it is likely to produce terror. We can reason, then, that the soothing *relief* that song brings to those loved by Zeus also results from their apprehending his judgment. This result credits the calming effect of Pindar's poetry to its audience's *cognitive* response, that is, upon their apprehending some truth.[39] The enemies of Zeus apprehend that they are detested and are accordingly seized by paralyzing fear. What do those who are soothed by song apprehend? That they are in Zeus's good graces, to be sure. But for the human audience in particular there is more to it.

Poetry, Pindar tells us, creates the memory of noble deeds.[40] Pindar's poetry does so by praising the victor and blessing him with good repute.[41] But Pindar goes further to add the conventional claim that his poetry confers immortality on its subject.[42] Poetry is like a splendid hall[43] in that it functions as a permanent and stable edifice. Poetry's power to soothe, then, would seem to consist in its granting the subject knowledge that he has the fame, the blessing of the gods, and the immortality that song can grant. Together, these narrow the anxiety relieved by poetry to nothing less than the fear of death. Poetry's therapeutic work is not accomplished by inducing diversion or forgetfulness. The victor does not momentarily *forget* his fear of death. Rather, it is allayed by a poetically induced confidence in his own immortality. Although it is specifically the victor who is soothed by poetry, Pindar tells us that his kinsmen are granted immortality by association: "nor does the dust bury the cherished glory of kinsmen."[44]

The theory of poetry that informs Pindar's persona as a poet underwrites some pointed claims to the superiority of his own poetry over his predecessors'. I have discussed some of the revisionary passages in which Pindar disputes rival versions of myths, including his well-known proposed correction of the Tantalus story and his dispute with the Homeric portrayal of Odysseus. Proposing a basis upon which a poet can challenge, and hope to surpass, his predecessors marks one of the innovations of Pindar's theory. Pindar's narrator can claim superiority over his predecessors without impugning the quality of Homer's or Hesiod's inspiration. Pindar's poet-

---

[39] Unlike in Hesiod, where poetry's therapeutic effect is not associated with its audience's knowledge nor with what they believe.

[40] *Nemean* 7. 14–17: "We know of a mirror for noble deeds in only one way, if, by the grace of Mnemosyne with the shining crown, one finds recompense for his labors in poetry's famous songs." See also *Isthmian* 7. 17–19: ". . . and mortals forget what does not attain poetic wisdom's choice pinnacle, yoked to glorious streams of verses."

[41] *Olympian* 7. 10.

[42] See *Olympian* 10. 91–96; *Pythian* 1. 92–100.

[43] *Olympian* 6. 1–7.

[44] *Olympian* 8. 79–80.

ics contributes an idea of the superior poet as the better *interpreter* of the Muse's messages. Of course, since the messages are conveyed in the privacy of inspiration, this explanation of superiority by itself can offer no criterion or way of telling who is the superior interpreter. Nevertheless, unlike both Homer and Hesiod, Pindar's poetics lend sense to his revisionist claims that some specifics of his predecessors' poems are erroneous. In general, it lends sense to the idea that, through no fault of the Muse, a poem may be wrong in the ways that a bad translation may be wrong. A poem can go wrong by translating a true and divine message into a generally intelligible poem that is false. Pindar's appeal to moral scruples to defend his criticism of his predecessors is designed to make him appear infallible, although it is fully adaptable to serve his own self-interest by providing a rationale for dogmatically upholding conventional values.

Pindar's poetry pretends to the kind of wisdom of men who solve oracle's riddles at the same time that it claims the authority of divinities who issue oracles. His poetry mobilizes this heterogeneous mix of forces in praise of victors, as it allies itself with the values of an aristocratic establishment. Pindar's poetics would insulate the poet from criticism of his inspiration and turn away any rival interpreter. With Pindar the fission is complete between two conceptions that Homeric poetics would keep fused. Homer subverts reflection that would separate issues of truth from those of meaning and interpretation; poetry conveys truths whose meaning requires no interpretation to grasp. Receiving truth and understanding it are one and the same process. Hesiod breaks the connection between poetry's truth and its significance, but he confines significance to his poetry's pleasurable effect. Pindar suppresses any question of challenging his account of the Muse's meaning, but he clearly separates receiving the Muse's truths from interpreting her meaning. Without disputing the truth of the poet's contribution, Socrates will ask what it means and how it should be interpreted.

Chapter Four

Socratic Poetics

SET AGAINST the background of the poets' theories of poetry, Plato's dialogues *Ion* and *Protagoras,* together with the *Apology,* can be shown to advance a revisionary Socratic poetics. Socrates' account undermines the general theme of discouraging interpretation that we found common to the poets' various theories of poetry. We shall find that Socrates' poetics discredits the inspired poets' claims to divine knowledge and topples the poet from sovereignty over his poetry's significance. Socrates' democratizing of poetry assigns the interpreter's task to audiences and supplies Socratic inquiry as the method for interpreting poetry. We have seen the notion of interpretation emerge in Pindaric poetics, but Pindar excluded all but the privileged poet from interpreting the Muse's words. Socrates, by contrast, provides a method that disciplines interpretation, makes it generally available to poetry's audience, and prevents it from being a mere instrument of the poet's authority. As we have already mentioned, the allegorical tradition had begun to undertake the task of interpreting the great poets, but as a way of maintaining the poets' authority in the face of new standards of conceptual thought.[1] Socratic poetics serves the more radical goal of denying that poetry's real value stems from something that the poet himself contributes.

This chapter approaches Socratic poetics from what I shall argue is an implicit attack on the Homeric theory of poetry in the *Ion* and a more general denial of the traditional Athenian view of poets as wise educators and privileged interpreters. By maintaining the traditional view that poetry harbors wisdom, but denying that either the poet or rhapsode grasps that wisdom, the *Ion* and *Apology* together pose the question of who is qualified to interpret poetry. In the next chapter, I suggest that Socrates begins to answer this question in his attack on sophistic poetics in the *Protagoras,* and in his interpretation of the Delphic oracle's pronouncement in the *Apology.*

The *Ion* introduces the first main themes of Socrates' account of poetry by disputing doctrines we found at the basis of Homeric poetics. Homer's theory credits the inspired poet and his audience with divine knowledge. On this Homeric theory, divine inspiration *consists in* knowledge. The Socratic

---

[1] See Introduction.

account champions the tradition where it credits poets with divine inspiration, but it rejects the Homeric claim that inspiration suffices for knowledge. On the Homeric theory, the divine knowledge poetry conveys is quasi-perceptual knowledge. By insisting that knowledge must instead be a form of *technê*, Socrates precludes the possibility that poetry conveys knowledge.

The *Ion*'s argument proceeds in three steps. The first argues that the possibility of the rhapsode's art being specialized as narrowly as Ion's implies that this art is not a *technê*, or mastery of a subject matter. The second introduces an idea of poetic inspiration consistent with Ion's specialized virtuosity and so extravagantly noncognitivist that it denies even that the poets speak their own verses. The *Ion*'s final portion poses a puzzle unsolved by commentators: it apparently opens by repeating the same question already settled in the first section, of whether Ion's performance of Homer exercises any *technê*. I shall suggest that the concluding section, despite appearances, does indeed advance the dialogue's argument. There, I shall suggest, Ion develops his position by proposing a more promising candidate for the rhapsode's *technê*: the art of persuasive speech. Ion's proposal, we shall see, elicits a different sort of Socratic response from any Socrates offered in the first part of the dialogue.

In the *Apology,* we shall see that Socrates elaborates and modifies the *Ion*'s account of poetic inspiration by maintaining explicitly what the *Ion* left as a mere possibility. In the *Ion*, Socrates argues that the rhapsode and poet lack knowledge or understanding of poetry. From this argument alone, it remains a question whether Socrates' view credits poetry with having any wisdom to offer or even with having any discoverable significance. The *Apology,* however, resolves this matter by accepting that poetry harbors divine wisdom and maintaining the need for interpretation in order to access such wisdom.

A Rhapsode's Knowledge

Socrates' interlocutor in the *Ion* enters fresh from his first prize performance of Homeric verse in a competition among rhapsodes held at a festival in Epidaurus. As a Homeric rhapsode, Ion is a professional performer and eulogist of Homeric poetry.[2] The dialogue's central argument begins only after Ion claims to know, not only Homer's verses, but also what the poet means.[3] The second of Ion's knowledge claims, which the *Ion* also characterizes as "knowledge of the poet's thought" fixes the target for Soc-

---

[2] On rhapsodes in general, see P. Murray, ed., *Plato on Poetry* (Cambridge 1996), pp. 96–99.

[3] *Ion* 530b10–c1.

rates' elenchic argument in the first of the *Ion*'s three main parts. Socrates does not question the breadth and accuracy of Ion's knowledge of Homeric verse. This technical mastery of a subject matter consists in nothing less than Ion's memory of the verses, and perhaps a good deal more.[4] He does, however, subject to Socratic inquiry Ion's claim to know Homer's thought. In place of the rhapsode's avowed knowledge of the poet's meaning, the *Ion*'s central passage (533d–536d) will introduce a Socratic theory of poetic inspiration that accounts for the rhapsode's success without crediting him with any knowledge beyond his knowledge of the poet's verse. In the light of this subsequent denial that the successful rhapsode either has or requires knowledge of the poet's thought, the question arises of why Socrates prompts Ion's claim to have such knowledge in the first place. Socrates elicits Ion's claim by adding to his interlocutor's boastful announcement of his victory at Epidaurus his own studiously excessive expression of admiration:

> You know, Ion, many times I've envied you rhapsodes your profession. Physically, it is always fitting for you in your profession to be dressed up to look beautiful as you can and at the same time it is necessary for you to be at work with poets—many fine ones, and with Homer above all, who's the best poet and the most divine—and you have to learn his thought, not just his verses! Now that is something to envy! (530b5–c1)

Socrates' grounds for prompting Ion's claim to understand Homer's thought are no less pretextual than his admiration is exaggerated. The subsequent argument leaves it unmistakable that Socrates' view of the rhapsode's profession emphatically denies that a rhapsode—even one as successful as Ion—has any need of knowledge of the poet's thought. So the *Ion* starts with a puzzle: why does Socrates encourage this vulnerable, self-congratulatory interlocutor to boast that he has "learned Homer's thought," a claim that, as the dialogue soon reveals, Socrates maintains is false?

Commentators who pass over this question may share the apparently commonsensical assumption, which Socrates voices and Ion finds convincing, that knowing what the poet means is an indispensable condition for the rhapsode's doing what he does well. Socrates concludes his praise of the rhapsode by summarizing its rationale:

> No one would ever get to be a good rhapsode if he didn't understand what is meant by the poet. A rhapsode must come to present the poet's thought to his audience; and he can't do that beautifully unless he knows what the poet means.[5]

[4] From the beginning, then, there is no question but that Socrates credits Ion with *some techné*, alluded to as Ion's knowledge of Homer's "verses" (τὰ ἔπη, 530c1).

[5] οὐ γὰρ ἂν γένοιτό ποτε ἀγαθὸς ῥαψῳδός, εἰ μὴ συνείη τὰ λεγόμενα ὑπὸ τοῦ ποιητοῦ. τὸν γὰρ ῥαψῳδὸν ἑρμηνέα δεῖ τοῦ ποιητοῦ τῆς διανοίας γίγνεσθαι τοῖς ἀκούουσι· τοῦτο δὲ καλῶς ποιεῖν μὴ γιγνώσκοντα ὅτι λέγει ὁ ποιητὴς ἀδύνατον (530c1–5).

But the middle portion of the *Ion* makes it clear that Socrates subscribes to no such assumption. He grants that Ion performs and eulogizes Homer's verses beautifully, but the sustained argument of much of the dialogue is devoted to disputing, and to replacing, the assumption that Ion's success as a rhapsode testifies to his having knowledge of Homer's thought. Socrates devotes the central portion of the *Ion* to introducing a noncognitive theory of poetic inspiration that accounts for the rhapsode's success in terms of divine inspiration alone. Ion's is a divine gift conveyed via the Muse and poet that, on Socrates' account, allows the rhapsode, as well as the inspired poet, to successfully perform verse he does not understand. Poetic inspiration is a state that incapacitates the rhapsode and poet for thought or knowledge. Plainly, then, Socrates himself rejects the apparently innocent notion (that he intimates above at 530c) that the rhapsode's talent depends on his knowledge of what the poet means. So our question does require an answer.

Various versions of a common approach to the *Ion* imply an answer that would amount to this: Socrates prompts Ion's claim as a pretext for attacking the value of poetry in general. This attack is directed not so much against Ion as it is against Homer and Homeric poetry. Commentators who take this approach assume that the arguments of the *Ion* contribute solely or primarily to advancing, in a preliminary way, the *Republic*'s banishment of poetry.[6] On this view, the *Ion* approaches the same issues as the *Republic*, and aims for the same results as the discussion in *Republic* 10, but it does so as if from a metaphysically neutral basis, unarmed with the theory of forms. On Janaway's version of this reading of the *Ion*, Socrates' argument aims to disparage poetry by establishing that poetry does not provide knowledge.[7] Janaway infers that poetry must be treated uniformly with its treatment in *Republic* 10, as affecting audiences deleteriously just because it alters their emotions and not their cognition.[8] I shall suggest, however, that attention to Socrates' argument in the *Apology* undermines Janaway's inference. That inference assumes that poetry cannot provide its audience with knowledge unless it is the product of a knowledgeable poet. In the *Apology* Socrates defends just the negation of this assumption. There, we shall see, he maintains that audiences can extract from poetry implications that the poet who composed them fails himself to grasp. In general, views like Janaway's that focus on the *Ion*'s anticipations of Plato's treatment of poetry in the *Republic* tend to underestimate the contributions to theorizing about poetry in other Socratic works, including the *Apology* and *Pro-*

---

[6] See, for example, P. Woodruff, *Plato, Two Comic Dialogues: Ion and Hippias Major* (Indianapolis, 1983), pp. 5–11; Ferrari 1989, pp. 108–10.

[7] C. Janaway, *Images of Excellence: Plato's Critique of the Arts* (Oxford, 1995), p. 14.

[8] See *Republic* 605b.

tagoras. As I shall show, in these works Socrates salvages the traditional fifth-century position that credits poetry with harboring wisdom of divine origin, but he rejects the further orthodoxy that credits poets themselves with having the knowledge that their poetry communicates. Together, the Socratic works *Apology* and *Protagoras* recommend a Socratic method of interpreting poetry that withholds attributions of knowledge to rhapsodes and poets.

Woodruff's version of the reading of *Ion* as a precursor to the *Republic* supposes that Ion serves as a stand-in for Homer, whose exalted status among Athenians somehow prevented Socrates from criticizing him directly.[9] On this account, we might say that Socrates prompts Ion's knowledge claim in order to humiliate Homer and disparage the value of Homer's poetry. I would suggest, however, that Socrates' position vis-à-vis Homer and Homeric poetry is more complex, not entirely negative, and more of a bona fide intellectual debate than this reading allows. I will argue, for example, that Socrates actually maintains the traditional attribution of wisdom to poetry, but disputes both the notions that the poet himself has the divine knowledge his poetry conveys, and that the audience can receive such knowledge from the poet simply by hearing the poetry. In disputing these ideas, Socrates does attempt to wrest from the poets the authority traditionally attributed to them, but he does so by engaging with the poets' own theories of poetry, with Homer's in particular.

An answer suggested by Vlastos's general conception of Socratic philosophy would lead us to focus on the character of Ion. Could it be that Socrates induces Ion to claim to know Homer's thought with an end to disclosing and improving his interlocutor's character?[10] The *Ion* supplies little of substance on which to base an answer. Ion lacks features that provide motivation for Socrates' examination of other interlocutors, such as Euthyphro or the politicians, poets, and craftsmen he examines in the *Apology*. Unlike the dogmatic and patricidal Euthyphro,[11] Ion's harmless boasts pose no threat to society. Ion and Euthyphro may share a certain naïveté,

---

[9] Woodruff 1983, pp. 5–11, a view also endorsed by I. Murdoch, *The Fire and the Sun: Why Plato Banished the Artists* (Oxford, 1977), p. 9.

[10] According to Vlastos, the twofold goal of the Socratic elenchus is "to discover how every human being ought to live *and* to test that single human being who is doing the answering—to find out if *he* is living as one ought to live" (G. Vlastos, "The Socratic Elenchus: Method Is All," in Vlastos 1994, p. 10).

[11] Like Aristophanes' Socrates, Euthyphro's way of thinking pits son against father. On Euthyphro's dogmatism see *Euthyphro* 4e–5a: "Whereas, by Zeus, Euthyphro, you think that your knowledge of the divine, and of piety and impiety, is so accurate that, when those things happen as you say, you have no fear of having acted impiously in bringing your father to trial? I should be of no use, Socrates, and Euthyphro would not be superior to the majority of men, if I did not have accurate knowledge of all such things."

but naïve as he may be, we shall find that Ion's objections to Socrates include two that Murdoch and Janaway endorse.[12] Ion, then, can be distinguished from Euthyphro by his displaying some grasp of Socrates' criticisms. Where Euthyphro demonstrates an incapacity to make progress beyond his initial appeal to the authority of his avowed unique connection to the divine, Ion responds to Socratic criticism by retreating (as we shall see) from his opening position that is informed mainly by Homeric poetics, to a version of a standard sophistical position in the third and final part of the dialogue.[13] As Ion differs from Euthyphro, he also lacks the reputation for wisdom and the theoretical pretensions that prompted Socrates' examination of the politicians, poets, and craftsmen in the *Apology,* and others elsewhere.[14] Rhapsodes, it appears, had a reputation for stupidity.[15] It is unclear, then, what feature of Ion's character might make him an interlocutor attractive to Socrates' inquiry.

A more satisfactory answer to this question of why Socrates induces Ion to claim to know what Homer means approaches the *Ion* as aimed specifically at criticizing features of the theory of poetry that our earlier discussion found poetically expounded in Homer. According to the Homeric theory, the poet is endowed with, and conveys to his audience, divine knowledge. Homer's poetics more generally supports the poet's authority as unquestionable by discouraging interpretation that would leave the poetry—and the poet's own interpretations—open to evaluation by his audiences. This Homeric theory of poetry allows, and indeed promotes, a complementary view of the rhapsode. The theory implies that the rhapsode, like the poet, simply in virtue of being inspired and transmitting inspiration to an audience, must also possess authoritative knowledge. Socrates rightly views Ion as an emblem (although not a self-conscious bearer) of this traditional view, which the *Ion* begins by introducing, and then sets out to evaluate. I would suggest, then, that Socrates induces Ion to claim that he has knowledge of the poet's thought in order to introduce for Socratic examination the traditional, Homeric view that poetic inspiration conveys divine knowledge. Socrates will argue that, although inspiration from the gods is necessary for poetry to harbor wisdom that the Homeric theory and tradition would have us find in poetry, this inspiration cannot suffice to convey knowledge.

---

[12] 540b: that Ion's *technē* is knowing what is appropriate for a man or woman to say (Murdoch 1977, p. 9); 531a: that specializing in Homer is "good enough" to count as knowledge (Janaway 1995, p. 14).

[13] Contrast Murray 1996, p. 98: "Ion himself is so stupid that he is not worth attacking."

[14] See *Apology* 21e–22e.

[15] See Murray 1996, p. 98, citing *Ion* 539e7 as evidence.

Ion's Virtuosity

Socrates poses a single question that challenges Ion's claim that he knows the meaning of Homer's verse and grasps the poet's thought:

> Are you so wonderfully clever about Homer alone—or about Hesiod and Archilochus?
> No, no. Only about Homer. That's good enough, I think. (531a1–4)

Ion's answer, Socrates will argue, is incompatible with his having the knowledge he claims. Socrates does not dispute the possibility that a rhapsode could specialize exclusively in Homeric poetry because he utterly lacks interest in any other poet. Since the dialogue introduces Ion as a champion among contesting rhapsodes, readers may presume that Ion's virtuosity does not signal some defect in his art, but is, rather, among its essential features. Socrates next argues that the rhapsode's art is not knowledge, that Ion lacks the technical or epistemic capacity that he would have if his claim to understand Homer's meaning were true. The fact that the rhapsode's art can be devoted exclusively to a single poet and remain inapplicable to all other poets implies, Socrates argues, that it is not a *techné*. The thesis Socrates will defend, then, is that Ion's specialized virtuosity excludes his art from being an epistemic or technical mastery. He will accordingly suggest that the explanation for Ion's successful career in the show business of a Homeric rhapsode must be something other than his possessing the knowledge that constitutes a *techné*.

The strategy of Socrates' argument in the first part of the *Ion* thus aims to locate the peculiarity of Ion's art in the rhapsode himself. From this subjectivist conclusion, Socrates will proceed directly to accommodate Ion's virtuosity with his own theory of poetic inspiration, and to undermine any pretension the poet has to wisdom. Socrates first argues that the peculiarity of Ion's virtuosity cannot be traced to any feature unique to Homer's poetry:

> Does Homer speak of any subjects that differ from those of all the other poets? Doesn't he mainly go through tales of war, and of how people deal with each other in society—good people and bad, ordinary folks and craftsmen? And of the gods, how *they* deal with each other and with men? And doesn't he recount what happens in heaven and hell, and tell of the births of gods and heroes? Those are the subjects of Homer's poetry-making, aren't they? (531c2–d2)

All of Homer's subject matter is common to some other poet. It follows that Ion's eccentric virtuosity does not accurately represent anything unique in Homer's *subject matter*. What Socrates infers, however, without additional argument, is that Ion's virtuosity accurately represents no peculiarity of Homer's poetry at all. Ion raises no complaint. Readers will wonder why Socrates considers only the possibility of a unique Homeric subject matter and disregards the fact that there are other types of features unique to Homeric poetry. Why, for example, couldn't Ion's talent spring from an understanding of the peculiar *artistry* with which Homer treats his unexceptional subject matter? Versions of this question, to which I shall return below, are salient in the final part of the *Ion*'s argument.

Socrates next considers the case for accounting for Ion's singular virtuosity by appealing to the unique value of Homer's poetry. Socrates has already declared Homer "the best poet and most divine."[16] Ion, of course, concurs with this assessment. Socrates nevertheless argues for rejecting Ion's suggestion that his virtuosity rests on the unique value of Homeric poetry. Ion contends that, where any other poet's verse has the same subject matter as Homer's, "Homer does it better."[17] Assuming that only one poet can be the best, these declarations of Homer's superiority promise to explain Ion's virtuosity in terms of his object's unique worth. But Socrates denies that appealing to knowledge of Homer's unique value can explain Ion's virtuosity. If Ion had knowledge of Homer's singularly superior value, he must have knowledge of other poets as well, since knowledge of Homer's superiority is comparative; it includes knowledge of other poets.[18] The limitations of Ion's virtuosity, then, are incompatible with his having knowledge of Homer's unique superiority. Ion's specialized virtuosity remains still to be explained:

> Then how in the world do you explain what I do, Socrates? When someone discusses another poet I pay no attention, and I have no power to contribute anything worthwhile: I simply doze off. (532b8–c2)

The fact that Ion's competence is confined to Homer implies, according to Socrates, that his rhapsodic art is not knowledge or a technical capacity:

> Anyone can tell that you are powerless to speak about Homer on the basis of knowledge or mastery. Because if your ability came by mastery, you would be able to speak about all the other poets as well. (532c5–8)

Here it remains somewhat unclear just how generally Socrates' thesis should be taken. Does he mean that in order to make *any* knowledgeable evaluation of Homer one must also be familiar with all other poetry? The lack of intervening argument suggests that the passage above may be taken merely to restate Socrates' previous claim about comparative evaluations.[19] Knowl-

---

[16] 530b9–10.
[17] 531d10.
[18] See the argument at 531d–532c.
[19] See Janaway 1995, pp. 17–18.

edge of Homer's comparative superiority to other poets requires a mastery that could be applied to evaluating those other poets. On this reading, Socrates makes no claim about noncomparative evaluations. But even if understood as applicable to evaluations generally, Socrates' claim still lacks the extravagant implication that anyone knowledgeable about Homer is familiar with all other poetry as well. To be knowledgeable in discussing and evaluating one painter calls on mastery of a discipline that is applicable to paintings generally. Socrates explicitly adds this principle of intradisciplinary assessment:

> Now take the whole of any other subject: won't it have the same discipline throughout? And this goes for every subject that can be mastered. (532d1–3)

There is no suggestion that one must be familiar with the work of more than one painter in order to acquire mastery of the discipline. Rather, Socrates' principle requires only that what one does acquire when one gains this mastery of the discipline is applicable throughout the subject, e.g., to all other paintings. The *Ion* cites additional examples of whole subjects, including sculpture and musical performance.[20] The idea of a "discipline" (*technê*) further suggests a standard of evaluation applicable throughout a given subject. This principle amounts to the requirement that evaluations be supportable by features that could be shared throughout a subject.

Here Socrates may be understood to invoke an informal general requirement for knowledge. The reason that no one can both speak knowledgeably about Homer's poetry and be unable to contribute anything about any other poetry is just that knowledge claims require backing by features that are applicable generally throughout a subject:

> Have you ever known anyone who is clever at explaining which statues are well made in the case of Daedalus, son of Metion, or Epeius, son of Panopeus, or Theodorus of Samos, or any other single sculptor, but who's lost when he's among the products of other sculptors, and dozes off and has nothing to say?[21] (533a6–b4)

The example of sculpture emphasizes the *peculiarity* of Ion's virtuosity. Only for poetry are there virtuoso experts like Ion, whose limitations result not from his having interest and familiarity confined to a single poet, but rather, from his being utterly *incapable* of bringing to any other poet

---

[20] See 532e–533b.

[21] Socrates makes the same point in a different way at the end of the *Symposium* (223d4–6) where he claims that "authors should be able to write both comedy and tragedy: the skillful (τέχνη) tragic dramatist should also be a comic poet." That is to say, if the poet comes by his talent through *knowledge*, that knowledge should be generally applicable throughout poetry's various genres.

the expertise and devotion he lavishes on Homer. Ion's virtuosity is the condition of a devotee of Homer who lacks the capacity to tell that Homer's poetry is superior to Hesiod's or even that Hesiod's verse compares more or less favorably with the verse of any other poet. Socrates' argument depends on the stronger claim that Ion is *incapable* of applying his gift to other poets. Were he merely unfamiliar with and uninterested in them, it would not follow that he lacks more generally applicable knowledge. In response to Socrates' remark that he performs *only* Homer, Ion says, "that's good enough, I think" (531a3–4). Commentators who sympathize with Ion and his claim to have knowledge applicable only to Homer[22] fail to see how absurdly narrow this specialized knowledge must be. How can one have knowledge of Homer without having knowledge that is more generally applicable? Homer's subject matter, like Hesiod's or Shakespeare's, includes not just particular facts, but general insights into, for example, human motivation. True to his unique calling as a *Homeric* rhapsode, Ion unwittingly views his own vocation through the eyes of Homeric poetics, according to which poetry transmits nothing general, but only quasi-perceptual knowledge—particular information or facts. But unless we ourselves adopt the Homeric theory, Socrates' requirement that Ion's knowledge be generally applicable seems quite reasonable.

At the close of this first section of the *Ion*, there remain alternatives still uncanvassed. Socrates has already exposed his reason for rejecting any suggestion that Ion's virtuosity betrays merely his private enthusiasm for Homer and Homeric poetry that happens to exhaust his interest in poetry and poets. The alternative Socrates will propose and defend in the dialogue's middle section accounts for Ion's virtuosity with a Socratic theory of poetic inspiration. There will remain for consideration in the *Ion*'s final part still another apparent alternative that returns us to Socrates' incomplete argument against allowing that Ion's specialization represents some unique feature of Homer's poetry, such as a unique Homeric verbal art.

Poetic Inspiration and Socratic Interpretation (533d–536d)

The *Ion*'s central section explains the singularity of the rhapsode's art by introducing a Socratic account of poetic inspiration. This account elaborates a rival to Homeric poetics by construing inspiration noncognitively and by confining the poet's contributions exclusively to his conveying his inspiration. Consequently, the theory also disposes of any question of Ion's—or anyone's—knowing what the poet means, since, according to the

[22] E.g., Benson 2000, p. 158.

Socratic account, there *is* nothing that the poet means; the poet serves as a purely passive channel for divine inspiration. Socrates replaces the Homeric idea that inspiration confers quasi-perceptual knowledge with the view that inspiration cannot be knowledge because it requires no epistemic mastery of a subject.

We can see how Homer and Socrates might be said to talk past each other in this dispute; we might attempt to defend Homer by suggesting that he and Socrates simply have different conceptions of knowledge. The divine knowledge that Homer's theory confers on poets applies no epistemic or technical mastery. The *Ion* does not argue against such a conception of knowledge, but simply replaces it with a rival Socratic view. Perhaps no such argument appears until Plato criticizes the view that perception is knowledge in the *Theaetetus*.[23] Presumably, though, Socrates maintains that a requirement for knowledge is that the knower grasp the meaning of what she knows, as this presumption propels his criticism of the poets' conception of themselves in the *Apology*.

The *Ion*'s highly poetic presentation of Socrates' theory invokes a figure that compares inspiration to the power of magnetic attraction transmitted from a permanently magnetic stone to each of a series of steel rings. These rings represent the Muse, poet, rhapsode, and audience linked by a force of attraction that passes through each of them:

> In the same way, the Muse makes some people inspired herself, and then through those who are inspired a chain of other enthusiasts is suspended. You know, none of the epic poets, if they're good, are masters of their subject; they are inspired, possessed, and that is how they utter all those beautiful poems. (533e3–8)

Socrates here suggests that Ion's being inspired accounts for both his singular Homeric art and for the lack of mastery or knowledge with which poets (and therefore, according to this theory also rhapsodes) perform. We will consider below the idea that inspiration is divine possession. First let us consider how, on the Socratic view, inspiration accounts for Ion's specialization. The specialization of a virtuoso rhapsode like Ion does not reflect any limitation in the Muse; on the contrary, the explanation for the singularity of Ion's specialization would seem to be the absence of any constraints that would limit the Muse's distribution of her gifts. The Muse distributes inspiration piecemeal so that Homer, for example, can be gifted with inspiration confined to epic poetry, and a lyric poet gifted in that genre only.[24] Ion, then, can inherit from Homer only the inspiration that went

---

[23] *Theaetetus* 151d–187a.

[24] See 534c2–4: "Each poet is able to compose beautifully only that for which the Muse has aroused him: one can do dithyrambs, another encomia, one can do dance songs, another epics and yet another iambics."

into Homeric epic. The Muse's choice of a specific poet or rhapsode is similarly unconstrained. So the rhapsode's singular specialization, like the poet's, excludes any requirement that those whom the Muse inspires must command a mastery that their poetry or poetic performance exercises. Socrates' theory permits the Muse to make some people inspired without regard, for example, to their resources for employing their gift.

This idea of inspiration as a gratuitously bestowed gift is of course sufficient to imply that the recipient of inspiration need not have knowledge or mastery of his subject. However, the idea that the Muse can inspire *anyone* is evidently exaggerated, even considering the example Socrates provides of Tynnichus "who never made a poem anyone would think worth mentioning, except for . . . almost the most beautiful lyric poem there is" (534d). The Muse favored the mediocre poet gratuitously. But this is far from suggesting that she might equally have triggered the production of the finest lyric poem by inspiring, say, a charioteer. It seems that not just anyone can be inspired, but only someone who is already a poet, or already a rhapsode. In the case of the rhapsode, Socrates alludes to what makes him susceptible to inspiration by distinguishing in the beginning of the dialogue between Ion's knowledge of Homer's verse and his (alleged) knowledge of Homer's thought. The rhapsode, we may infer, must have knowledge of Homer' verse (that is, have the verses memorized) in order for him to be inspired by the Muse with whatever it is that inspiration adds to this knowledge. Analogously, we must make a distinction in the case of the poet between a talent that makes him susceptible to inspiration and the Muse's gift of inspiration. It is clear that Socrates' theory of poetic inspiration is compatible with the distinction we noted in the case of the rhapsode: Ion's successful performance of Homer depends on his knowledge of the verse and on his position on the same chain of inspiration that connects Homer to the Muse. The question remains of how precisely to characterize an analogous distinction for poets.

One current answer proposes that inspiration contributes not what is true or wise in poetry, but only what is aesthetically valuable or moving.[25] This view does justice to the fact that Socrates seems to restrict inspiration to explaining superhuman excellence in human production, but it cannot account for another feature of Socrates' view. According to the Socratic theory, only poets are inspired. Sculptors, flute players, painters, and others who satisfy the modern conception of an artist are excluded from inspiration; their arts are *technai*.[26] But Socrates suggests no reason why the work of sculptors and painters cannot be aesthetically beautiful, and indeed, it would be unreasonable to exclude them from having such beauty.

---

[25] See Janaway 1995, ch. 1, esp. pp. 33–35.
[26] 532e–533b (*technên*, 532e4).

In the Socratic theory, then, inspiration does not contribute to poetry's purely *aesthetic* value. This point is crucial for understanding that Socrates' interest in the *Ion* and elsewhere is not aesthetics in general, but specific to poetry and its unique connection to the divine. For an answer to the question of what ingredient inspiration does contribute to the poet we must look to the *Apology*'s treatment of poetry, to which we shall turn shortly.

Before doing that, we need to consider Socrates' identification of inspiration with a state of "possession." This feature of Socrates' theory in the *Ion* provides his rationale for denying that those gifted with inspiration have knowledge, and consequently also the *Ion*'s primary reason for rejecting the Homeric view that inspiration confers divine knowledge:

> For a poet is an airy thing, winged and holy, and he is not able to make poetry until he becomes inspired and goes out of his mind and his intellect is no longer in him. As long as a human being has his intellect in his possession he will always lack the power to make poetry or sing prophesy. (534b3–7)

Not only is intellectual mastery not necessary for poets, but the gift of inspiration is incompatible with the poet's being at all engaged intellectually. As the *Ion* presents this account of inspiration, the poet is utterly passive when he appears most creative:

> The god takes their intellect away . . . so that we who hear should know that they are not the ones who speak those verses that are of such high value, for their intellect is not in them: the god himself is the one who speaks, . . . (534c7–d4)

Like prophets or oracles, the poet does not author his poetry; he is not the speaker of the verse that the Muse sings with his voice. The poet, then, contributes little more than amplification to an inaudible divine signal. Socrates here denies not only that the poet knows what he is saying, but also that it is the poet who says it. On Socrates' view, poetic inspiration is thoroughly noncognitive. The Muse speaks the poet's verses through the poet. The poet does not speak his verse any more than a radio speaks the voices it broadcasts. The example of Tynnichus, which we discussed earlier, confirms that "these beautiful poems are . . . divine and from the gods."[27] So, the inspired poet lacks not only knowledge of what his poems means, but even knowledge of what he says. The poet in this way differs from the rhapsode who can have knowledge of what Homeric verse says without knowing what it means. The *Ion* maintains that "poets are nothing but representatives of the gods, possessed by whoever possesses

---

[27] 534e3–4.

them."[28] Although Homer, Hesiod, and Pindar each in their different ways depicted the poet as standing in a privileged relation to the divine (the Homeric poet has divine knowledge; Hesiod's Muses breathe into him a divine voice; Pindar views the poet as inspired with the Muse's oracle), Socrates seems to be one of the first to depict the poet as in a state of ecstatic possession, comparable to the Bacchic Corybantes (534a).[29] As we shall see, however, there are reasons to think that the *Ion*'s account of the poet's utter passivity to some extent exaggerates Socrates' view.

Socrates characterizes the inspired poet's possession as a paralytic passivity that confines his role to one of uncomprehending transmitter of divine signals. He characterizes the rhapsode's possession, by contrast, as a more active state. Unlike the poet, the rhapsode speaks in his own voice, albeit in a state of delusion. When performing scenes of heroic daring or portraying victims of loss, his soul "believes he is in Troy." His "hair stands on end with fear and [his] heart jumps" when he tells a frightening or awful tale because he is in the delusional state that is the rhapsode's analogue to the poet's possession.[30] As Ion himself notes, his deluded condition does not prevent his lucid activity as shrewd entrepreneur; his communication of delusional enthusiasm goes on all the while he gauges his audience's emotional response and attends to collecting the cash:

> You see I must keep my wits and pay close attention to them: if I start them crying, *I* will laugh as I take their money, but if *they* laugh, I shall cry at having lost money. (535e3–6)

The rhapsode's audience—the final iron ring in the chain transmitting the god's magnetic force—enter into a temporary delusional state induced by the rhapsode's performance. Though neither the rhapsode nor his audience share the poet's paralytic state, Socrates characterizes all three as out of their right minds.[31] Here we have the foundation for the *Republic*'s view that poetry has unavoidable, psychologically devastating effects. But we need to guard against making too smooth a transition from the *Ion* to the *Republic*. We have already alluded to a point that turns out to signal a deep

---

[28] 534e4–5.

[29] See E. Tigerstedt, *Plato's Idea of Poetical Inspiration* (Helsinki, 1969), p. 26 , and "*Furor Poeticus:* Poetic Inspiration in Greek Literature before Democritus and Plato," *Journal of the History of Ideas* 31 (1970), pp. 163–78. Democritus too emphasized the poet's *enthousiasmos* in a theory of poetry now lost to us (see DK 68 B17–18; Most 1999, p. 339).

[30] See 535c. *Pace* Janaway 1995, pp. 21–22, Socrates avoids the modern question of how an audience can coherently fear what is fictional. The modern problem emerges from the apparent incoherence in fearing what one knows is not real. Ion's case different; given his (albeit delusional) belief that he is in Troy, his fear is absolutely rational.

[31] See 534b; 535d.

break between the *Ion* and Plato's discussion in the *Republic*. The Socratic psychology of poetic experience links belief with emotion in a way that Plato emphatically does not. On the Socratic view, even the emotions the rhapsode experiences when in the state of delusional inspiration are rational in that they are consistent with his beliefs; Ion *believes* he is present at a frightening situation in Troy, and so he is afraid:

> . . . doesn't your soul, in its enthusiasm, believe that it is present at the actions you describe, whether they're in Ithaca or in Troy or wherever the epic actually takes place?
>
> What a vivid example you've given me, Socrates! I won't keep secrets from *you*. Listen, when I tell a story that's frightening or awful, my hair stands on end with fear and my heart jumps. (535c2–8)

In *Republic* 10, on the other hand, Plato will make it clear that on his view poetic imitation affects even the best natures by encouraging emotions and attitudes that are inconsistent with the auditor's beliefs. Poetry increases the power of one's desires for excessive emotion, and eventually changes one's values by eradicating one's former beliefs.[32]

The *Ion* is standardly interpreted as advancing an uncompromising hostility to poetry. Commentators infer this hostility from Socrates' criticism of Ion's—and the poets'—claims to have knowledge or understanding. But this inference is too hasty. G. Ferrari, for example, interprets the *Ion* as condemning poetry as thin in content and as mere performance that should be evaluated and interpreted not according to the meaning of its verse, but only according to its immediate theatrical effects.[33] Ferrari ascribes to Socrates a view that reduces poetry's primary value to entertainment. Again, this interpretation takes the *Ion*'s denial that the poet and rhapsode possess knowledge to imply that poetry has only inspirational, and therefore paltry, value. This alleged implication is not contradicted in the *Ion*, but neither is it necessarily implied. The *Apology*, I will now suggest, undermines it with the claim that, despite the poet's lack of understanding, poetry itself has wisdom or meaning.

The *Apology*'s main passage for our topic (Socrates' examination of the poets at 22a–c) contributes part of Socrates' account of his successful quest to solve the riddle posed by the Delphic oracle's pronouncement that no man is wiser than he is. The poets are the second of the three groups of reputedly wise Athenians whom Socrates questions in an effort to solve the puzzle posed by the oracle. Socrates first turns to the reputedly wise politi-

---

[32] See esp. 605b2–c4; 606b5–8; 606d1–4; 605b2–6; and D. Scott's lucid discussion in "Platonic Pessimism and Moral Education," *Oxford Studies in Ancient Philosophy* 17 (1999), pp. 34–36.

[33] Ferrari 1991, p. 96.

cians, whom he finds utterly without resource to support their reputation for wisdom. When Socratic inquiry calls upon them to reveal the basis of their reputation, they evidently can invoke nothing whatever—except for their reputation itself.[34] After the politicians, Socrates turns to the reputedly wise poets.

The reputation for wisdom that poets enjoyed depended not on current political popularity, but on the traditionalist attitudes (typified by the attitude that prompted Aristophanes twenty-four years earlier) that included a view of the poets as founts of time-tested wisdom, and poetry as suitable for the moral instruction of youth. Socrates discovers, for reasons unrelated to the politicians' deficiency in wisdom, that his second group of interlocutors poses no threat to the oracle's generalization either:

> So, taking up the poems of theirs that seemed to me to have been most carefully elaborated by them, I asked them what they meant, that I might at the same time learn something from them. Now I am ashamed to tell you the truth, gentlemen; but still it must be told. For there was hardly a man present, one might say, who would not speak better than they about the poems they themselves had composed. So again in the case of the poets also I presently recognized this, that what they composed they composed not by wisdom, but by nature and because they were inspired, like the prophets and givers of oracles; for these say many fine things, but know none of the things they say; it was evident to me that the poets too had experienced something of this same sort.[35]

The *Apology* replaces the *Ion*'s model of the poet as a passive channel. Here, poets are credited with composing their poems, and they are, as Socrates implies, equipped to compose them with greater or lesser care.[36] Like the *Ion*, however, the *Apology* disputes that the poet's gift enables him to grasp his poetry's meaning. The test by which Socrates settles the question of whether poets are worthy of their reputation for wisdom assesses the poet's ability to elucidate the significance of his own verse. Socrates argues from the assumption which he shares with the traditionalist (and with his inter-

---

[34] See *Apology* 21b–e.

[35] 22b3–c4: ἀναλαμβάνων οὖν αὐτῶν τὰ ποιήματα ἅ μοι ἐδόκει μάλιστα πεπραγματεῦσθαι αὐτοῖς, διηρώτων ἂν αὐτοὺς τί λέγοιεν, ἵν᾽ ἅμα τι καὶ μανθάνοιμι παρ᾽ αὐτῶν. αἰσχύνομαι οὖν ὑμῖν εἰπεῖν, ὦ ἄνδρες, τἀληθῆ· ὅμως δὲ ῥητέον. ὡς ἔπος γὰρ εἰπεῖν ὀλίγου αὐτῶν ἅπαντες οἱ παρόντες ἂν βέλτιον ἔλεγον περὶ ὧν αὐτοὶ ἐπεποιήκεσαν. ἔγνων οὖν αὖ καὶ περὶ τῶν ποιητῶν ἐν ὀλίγῳ τοῦτο, ὅτι οὐ σοφίᾳ ποιοῖεν ἃ ποιοῖεν, ἀλλὰ φύσει τινὶ καὶ ἐνθουσιάζοντες ὥσπερ οἱ θεομάντεις καὶ οἱ χρησμῳδοί· καὶ γὰρ οὗτοι λέγουσι μὲν πολλὰ καὶ καλά, ἴσασιν δὲ οὐδὲν ὧν λέγουσι. τοιοῦτόν τί μοι ἐφάνησαν πάθος καὶ οἱ ποιηταὶ πεπονθότες·

[36] The *Ion* presents a more extreme version of the poet's passivity, I would suggest, because of its particular focus on the Homeric theory of poetry, which, as we have seen, emphasizes the poet's role as conveyor of divine knowledge. The *Apology*, by contrast, focuses on poets and poetry more generally.

locutor), that there is wisdom in the verses the poet composes. His conclusion, that the poets compose "not by wisdom, but by nature and because they are inspired" (22b9–c1), invokes a principle to the effect that the author of any wisdom in poetry can understand that wisdom. The latter principle seems to be reasonable enough. The assumption that there is some wisdom in poetry is confirmed by Socrates' remark that the poets, like seers, "say many fine (*kala*) things without understanding them" (22c2–3). The adjective *kalos* often, but not always, reaches beyond the purely aesthetic to express a moral fineness.[37] Here, it would seem that it does refer to moral wisdom; Socrates compares the poet to the prophet or seer, and it is divine wisdom, not a purely aesthetic quality, that characterizes the seer's, and thus by implication the poet's pronouncements. It seems, then, that *poetry*'s moral fineness accounts for the poets' reputation for themselves being wise. Socrates' conclusion, that such a reputation is undeserved, implies that a poet cannot have authored the wisdom in the poetry he composes. Of course, Socrates does not deny that some poet could also coincidentally be a successful interpreter of his own compositions. He does claim, however, that whatever enables the poets to compose poetry adds nothing to their capacity to interpret their verse and know what it means. The inspired poets' role in the creation of poetry, then, cannot be as author of any wisdom implicit in their verse. The poets' presumption to have the wisdom that they merely convey and do not themselves grasp amounts to a false pretension to have divine wisdom. We now have, then, an answer to our question of what precisely inspiration contributes to poetry: in the *Apology* Socrates restricts poetic inspiration to account for just the wisdom or moral insight that poetry is traditionally thought to harbor.

Two crucial points, then, emerge from the *Apology* and are consistent with the *Ion*: (1) Socrates countenances the traditional view that there *is* wisdom originating from a divine source in truly inspired poetry, and (2) this wisdom is not immediately available to the audience, or poet, but *requires an act of interpretation to extract it*. The first point reflects the traditionalist side of the Socratic view of poetry. The second, that an act of interpretation is necessary to extract poetry's wisdom, is an idea that, although not original to Socrates as such, emerges here with a particular emphasis; since the poets cannot interpret their own poems, we are left wondering who *can* give an account of a poem's meaning. The rhapsode may claim authority as an interpreter, but as the *Ion* argues, he too lacks the knowledge required for understanding a poem's meaning.

In the context of what I have suggested is Socrates' agonistic relationship with the Homeric theory of poetry, the call for interpretation and the question of who is the qualified interpreter have radically antitraditionalist

---

[37] See Woodruff 1983, pp. 42–43.

implications. As we have seen, Homeric, Hesiodic, and Pindaric poetics each in their different ways attempts to deflect interpretation and in this way preserve the poet's unquestionable authority. The Socratic emphasis on the necessity of interpretation attempts to subvert the power and authority the poets originally attributed to themselves, and that they in fact enjoyed in fifth-century Athens when they were conventionally viewed as wise men and teachers. Hesiod's disavowal of knowledge does not in fact allow him to escape Socrates' censure. As we have seen, the Hesiodic therapeutic of poetry may deny that the poet has wisdom, but it serves ultimately as an attempt to deflect interpretation of poems in which the author nevertheless engages in a form of didacticism.

The Rhapsode's Speech (536d–542b)

In the next chapter we shall turn to questions concerning the particular nature of Socratic interpretation. First, however, let us return to the *Ion*'s concluding section. When Socrates' presentation of his own theory of poetic genius comes to a close, Ion remains unconvinced:

> You're a good speaker, Socrates. Still I would be amazed if you could speak well enough to convince me that I am possessed or crazed when I praise Homer. (536d4–6)

Persuading Ion was, of course, incidental to Socrates' aims in introducing his theory of poetic inspiration. But the formulation of Ion's protest exposes something more than Ion's own philosophical deficiency. Its emphasis on the topic of persuasive speech also signals the direction that the argument will take for the remainder of the dialogue. This third part of the *Ion* raises a puzzle that has not yet been solved by commentators. In this section, Socrates demands that Ion specify his own particular *techné* from among the many included in Homer's complex subject matter. After rejecting the navigator, doctor, and others, Ion brings the dialogue to a close with his claim that he possesses the *techné* of a general. This outcome of the *Ion*'s final line of argument has governed commentators' standard view that the dialogue's denouement merely displays the ease with which Socrates forces his hapless interlocutor to cling to a position that even he must understand is utterly absurd. Those who disparage the *Ion* for casting so inept a dialectician as Socrates' interlocutor find Ion's claim to have mastered the skill of a general merely dim. I shall suggest, however, that Ion's remarks at the opening of this section provide a hint that leads to a more promising interpretation of Ion's final claim, and to a resolution to the puzzle of why Ion chooses to count the general's *techné* as his own.

Socrates resumes the dialectic with a new question:

On which of Homer's subjects do you speak well? (536e1–2)

Socrates' question presupposes that the Homeric poems treat an inventory of discrete *technai*. Socrates' initial exchange with Ion on the question treats it as having asked Ion to specify the subjects on which he speaks knowledgeably. Homer's subjects include charioteering, divination, and fishing. There are no rhapsodes in the Homeric poems, but were Ion to appeal to some of the many Homeric poet-figures to specify his *techné*, for example to the bards Phemius and Demodocus in the *Odyssey*, he would be no further than he was at the start of the dialogue when he claimed to have acquired the poet's knowledge. Ion concedes that he cannot match most typical professionals' expertise:

> Should we say it's for a fisherman's profession or a rhapsode's to tell whether or not he [Homer] describes this beautifully and well? That's obvious, Socrates. It's for a fisherman's. (538d4–6)

Socrates persists in pressing Ion to specify which passages in Homer the rhapsode's art qualifies him to evaluate more competently than anyone else. Instead of doing so, Ion makes a start at advancing the argument, despite his ambitious but erroneous reply: "all of them" (539e6). Of course, Ion's prior concessions already established that this reply is false, as Socrates points out before the rhapsode's position takes a more promising turn:

> But then what sort of thing will a rhapsode know, if not everything? My opinion, anyhow, is that he'll know what it's fitting for a man or a woman to say—or for a slave or a freeman, or for a follower or a leader. (540b2–5)

Ion here tantalizingly verges on launching an idea of "fitting" speech that would have him claim insight into the appropriate relation between men and women of every social station and their speech. Iris Murdoch would have the rhapsode hold this ground by specifying as the rhapsode's competence "a general knowledge of human life" that is specialized only in combination with technical knowledge of poetry to yield "the humane judgment of the literary man."[38] Here, however, Socrates resists Ion's effort to turn the argument, without yet fully exposing his reasons for resisting. If the rhapsode's art, according to Ion, qualifies him to supply fitting speech, it fails to do so in all circumstances, as Socrates' first two examples illustrate. The rhapsode agrees that he does not command the speech fitting a navigator in circumstances "when he's at sea and his ship is hit by a storm" (540b6–8), nor of a doctor ". . .when he's in charge of a sick man . . . " (540c1–2), nor what a slave who is a cowherd should say about his expertise, nor what a woman who spins yarns should say "about

[38] Murdoch 1977, p. 9.

working with wool" (540c68). At last, it is the case of the general that elicits from Ion a novel response:

> And what a man should say, if he's a general, to encourage his troops?
> Yes! That's the sort of thing a rhapsode will know. (540d2–3)

It may be that we should dismiss the rhapsode's claim to command the general's *technê* as merely confused. In any case, Ion cannot be absolved of confusion, nor can his selection of the general's *technê* be explained by adopting Janaway's generous effort to find backing for Ion's claim in the great number of passages that concern generalship in the *Iliad* and which the champion rhapsode proudly claims to know.[39] The skill of the navigator is a second *technê* that is roughly comparable to generalship in the extent to which it is described by Homer, and we noted that the navigator's skill is in the list of special skills that Socrates proffers and Ion explicit disavows. So the question remains unresolved of what accounts for Ion's claim to have the general's *technê*. My own suggestion follows the hint that Ion dropped earlier when he revealed his preoccupation with persuasive speech. Ion claims to have the *technê* that a general exercises in knowing what to say "to encourage his troops." His response suggests that he is claiming not that he knows what to say to troops about military strategy, but that he possesses the general's skills of persuasive speech. Socrates put his interlocutor at a loss to explain why a general like himself has not been entrusted with any army. He then concludes with this substantive objection that would apply to anyone claiming to command a *technê* of persuasion:

> You aren't even willing to tell me what it is that you're so wonderfully clever about, though I've been begging you for ages. Really, you're just like Proteus, you twist up and down and take many different shapes, till finally you've escaped me altogether by turning yourself into a general, so as to avoid proving how wonderfully wise you are about Homer. (541e4–542a1)

Socrates' rejection of claims to have a *technê* of persuasive speech is of course familiar from his repeated contrast of sophists with artisans who have an actual, and not merely apparent, *technê*.[40] Ion's claim to possess the persuasive skill of a general evidently falls under the same rubric Socrates applies to the utterly elusive, since merely apparent, *technê* of the sophists. The same should apply to supposing that there is a *technê* of Homer's unique artistry concerning the uniquely compelling and beautiful way that

---

[39] Janaway 1995, p. 27.

[40] Socrates' discussion of the sophist Evenus at *Apology* 19e–20c, for example, treats the sophist's claim to possess the *technê* of virtue with a strong irony (see especially 20c1–3) that has the effect of comparing him unfavorably to those who possess arts like horse breeding or farming (20b1–2).

Homeric verse presents its subject matter (that is, the unique way that Homeric speech is persuasive). Socrates would not hesitate to direct the same objection he applies in the case of Ion's claim to have the general's *techné*: there exists no *techné* of persuasive speech apart from knowledge of a particular subject matter. In other words, one cannot, on the Socratic view, be a truly (and not merely apparently) persuasive speaker without knowledge of the subject matter about which one is speaking. On Socrates' view, then, the general does not possess any *techné* of persuasive speech separable from his knowledge of military strategy or some other particular subject matter. Similarly, if Homer's and the rhapsode's *techné* is one of a unique, "Homeric artistry," then it must be said to be no *techné* at all: according to Socrates, there can be no *techné* of Homer's verbal artistry apart from knowledge of the particular subject matters with which his poetry concerns itself.

We have found that the *Apology* and the *Ion* implicitly engage the Homeric theory of poetry, in particular its identification of the poet's inspiration with knowledge. By denying that the Homeric conception of quasi-perceptual knowledge counts as knowledge at all, Socrates firmly separates poetic inspiration from knowledge, which according to Socrates must be a type of *techné*. In arguing that divine inspiration, not knowledge, provides the explanation for the rhapsode's success and for the poet's ability to compose poetry that contains some wisdom, Socrates reveals that the gift of inspiration does not provide its recipients with the ability to give an account of poetry's meaning or to extract any wisdom that poetry may contain. As usual, Socrates leaves us (quite deliberately, I would suggest) with a set of questions: Who *is* the qualified interpreter of poetry? What are the desiderata of a good interpretation? By focusing our attention on these questions of interpretation, and on the necessity of interpretation, Socrates undermines Homer's, Hesiod's, and Pindar's shared aim of maintaining authority and their common tactic of deflecting interpretation of their poetry. In the next chapter I shall suggest how Socrates begins to answer these questions in a Socratic poetics that would supplant the poet's theories and overcome their resistance to interpretation.

Chapter Five _____

Toward a Model of Socratic Interpretation

WE HAVE SEEN how the *Ion* challenges the Homeric conception of the poet as possessor and conveyer of divine knowledge, and how the *Apology* portrays Socrates as subverter of the poets' own authority in matters of interpretation. In the *Apology*, Socrates concurs with the traditional presumption that poetry encodes god-sent wisdom at the same time he disputes the tradition that credits that wisdom to poets. Socrates implies that the qualified interpreter, unlike the poet, can extract poetry's wisdom, but the *Apology* does not illustrate this hermeneutical enterprise with a specific example in which we may glimpse Socrates demonstrating his method of eliciting the meaning of some particular work of poetry. The one illustration of Socratic interpretation that the *Apology* does provide adapts Socratic hermeneutics to interpret nothing less than the Delphic oracle. As I shall show, Socrates' interpretation of the oracle illustrates the Socratic approach to interpreting a divinely inspired text. First, however, I shall turn to the *Protagoras,* where Socrates supplies an extended interpretation of a well-known poem by Simonides.[1] Unfortunately, Socrates' dialectical position in the *Protagoras* complicates the task of reading his interpretation as an illustration of Socratic poetics. His reading of Simonides' poem parodies sophistic methods of literary criticism so extravagantly that we may be tempted to dismiss it as mere pastiche. Doing so would prevent us from seeing that, in Socrates' caricature of sophistical methods of literary criticism and in his ridicule of their faulty hermeneutical assumptions, the *Protagoras* should be taken to illustrate the contrasting method and opposed assumptions of Socratic interpretation.

To be sure, Socrates' performance as a critic is deeply ironic. Commentators have been correct in their widely shared view that the episode attacks sophistical interpretive practices with an attempt to outdo the sophists at their own game. The interpretation Socrates presents is strained, anachro-

---

[1] As we shall see, Socrates' position here, as in the *Apology* and *Ion,* remains firmly distinct from Plato's well-known critique of the poets. The *Protagoras's* views are not informed by the *Republic's* ethical and metaphysical arguments against the value of poetry (the occurance of μιμεῖσθαι at 348a3 notwithstanding [see Carson 1992, p. 111]). This may be taken to supply an additional argument for including the *Protagoras* among either the early or transitional dialogues. See T. Irwin, *Plato's Moral Theory* (Oxford, 1977), p. 292. On the chronology of the Platonic dialogues in general, see L. Brandwood, "Stylometry and chronology," in R. Kraut, ed., *The Cambridge Companion to Plato* (Cambridge, 1992), pp. 90–120.

nistic, and employs dubious arguments to ascribe to Simonides philosophical theses that have only the most tenuous connection to what the poem
literally says.[2] These features suggest that Socrates' interpretation aims
merely to ridicule Protagoras and to demonstrate Socrates' avowed con-
tention here that all discussions aimed to establish conclusions that identify a poet's meaning are fruitless. But scholars have also had to face a difficulty. Socrates presents his interpretation as the product of his serious
study of Simonides' poem. This suggests not only that his interpretation
has a serious intent, but also that interpreting poetry could form part of his
life's project, which is, as we know from the *Apology,* philosophical inquiry.
In order to reconcile Socrates' serious intent with the manifestly comic elements of his interpretation and with his remarks that appear to condemn
literary criticism as a fruitless enterprise, scholars have been obliged to
argue either that Socrates is disingenuous when he claims to have taken the
poem seriously,[3] or that the extravagant interpretation should indeed be

[2] As most commentators agree. See C. C. W. Taylor, *Plato, Protagoras* (Oxford, 1976),
p. 146: "Once again, Socrates' assimilation of the poet's thought to one of his own theses involves a blatant perversion of the plain sense of the poem." G. Vlastos, *Socrates: Ironist and
Moral Philosopher* (Ithaca, 1991), p. 136: "Returning to his exegesis of the poem of Simonides
after spinning out this pseudo-historical extravaganza, [Socrates] resumes his manhandling of
the text, torturing crypto-Socratic wisdom out of it." D. Frede, "The Impossibility of Perfection: Socrates' Criticism of Simonides' Poem in the *Protagoras,*" *Review of Metaphysics* 39
(1986), pp. 729–53, claims that Socrates countenances the doctrines he attributes to Simonides, but that he "imposes, consciously and forcefully, these doctrines on the poem"
(740) and has to "distort the text to serve his own purposes" (737); M. Demos, *Lyric Quotation in Plato* (New York, 1999), p. 23: "[His] convoluted defense . . . becomes an oppor-
tunity for Socrates to voice his own philosophical views although they are attributed to Simonides." Harriott 1969, p. 145: in giving his interpretation Socrates "is dishonest and
quibbling." See also: J. Adam and A. M. Adam, *Platonis Protagoras* (Cambridge, 1928), p.
194; A. Carson, "How Not to Read a Poem: Unmixing Simonides From *Protagoras,*" *CP* 87
(1992), p. 110: "[Socrates and Protagoras] so thoroughly misquote, misconstrue, and mis-
represent [Simonides' poem] that most readers are left wondering why philosophers bother
to read poetry at all"; G. Ferrari, "Plato and Poetry," in G. A. Kennedy, ed., *The Cambridge
History of Literary Criticism. Volume One: Classical Criticism* (Cambridge, 1989), pp. 102–
3: "[Socrates] has reinterpreted the poem as if it were itself the kind of philosophical argument to which it provokes him. . . . But a poem is not meant to be a set of opinions . . . ; it
is meant for performance." See also P. Friedländer, *Plato: The Dialogues,* vol. 2 (New York,
1964), pp. 24–25; H. Gundert, "Die Simonides-Interpretation in Platons *Protagoras,*" in
Hermeneia: Festschrift Otto Regenbogen (Heidelberg, 1952), pp. 71–74; W. R. M. Lamb,
Plato: Protagoras (New York, 1924), pp. 88–89; H. D. Verdam, "De carmine Simonideo
quod interpretatur Plato in Protagoro dialogo," *Mnemosyne* 56 (1928), p. 306; L. Woodbury,
"Simonides on Arete," *TAPA* 84 (1953), pp. 141–50. Exceptions to the scholarly consensus
are: W. Donlan, "Simonides Fr. 4D and P. Oxy. 2432," *TAPA* 100 (1969), p. 75; D. Babut,
"Simonide moraliste," *Rev. Etud. Grecq.* 88 (1975), p. 44, and to a certain extent, H. Parry,
"An Interpretation of Simonides 4 (Diehl)," *TAPA* 96 (1965), p. 315.

[3] Ferrari 1989, p. 101.

taken seriously.[4] For reasons I shall discuss below, neither of these approaches has yielded entirely satisfactory results. Here I shall propose an alternative, indirect path to reconciling the conflicting demands of this episode. On my reading, the interpretation Socrates supplies aims to be manifestly perverse and sophistic, but just because it is deliberately anti-Socratic, it draws the outlines of what a truly Socratic interpretation would look like. Indirectly, Socrates gestures toward an antisophistic approach to interpreting Simonides' poem. To see how Socrates' reading of Simonides' poem illustrates Socratic interpretation, we must look beyond the *Protagoras* to the wider context provided by Socrates' view of poetry in the *Apology* and *Ion*. This tacit, but nonetheless distinctively Socratic, approach to literary criticism in the *Protagoras* will be seen not to condemn the interpretation of poetry as futile and trivial, but to illustrate and elaborate the position we found in the *Apology* and *Ion*. In the *Protagoras*, Socrates perseveres in his aim to retrieve the hermeneutical task from poets, sophists, and their coterie. He appropriates interpretation as a task that is itself properly philosophical and fully within the competence of poetry's audience. In the course of Socrates' retrieval of the interpreter's task, he revises the principles and resets the purposes of interpretation.

Protagoras as Critic

The Simonides episode begins with Protagoras's proposal to open what he calls a discussion of virtue "translated into the sphere of poetry" (339a7). Protagoras's speech is in fact his attempt to subvert the moral authority that fifth-century Athens traditionally granted to the poet and to claim that authority for his own. Plato illustrates Protagoras's skill at the manipulative appropriation of power. Protagoras makes a show of celebrating the Athenian mentality that assigns to the interpretation of poetry pride of place in the intellectual training of the educated classes: "the greatest part of a man's education is to be in command of poetry, by which I mean the ability to understand the words of the poets, to know when a poem is correctly composed and when not, and to know how to analyze a poem and to respond to questions about it" (339a1–5). These general remarks anticipate Protagoras's effort to exploit, for purposes that do not honor tradition, the traditionalist stance that relies on poetry for moral instruction. Protagoras would appropriate for *himself* and his own sophistry authority over poetry's interpretation. Protagoras thus takes up a contest with high

[4] See Frede 1986; N. Pappas, "Socrates' Charitable Treatment of Poetry," *Philosophy and Literature* 13 (1989), pp. 248–61; Demos 1999, all of whose views I discuss in more detail below.

stakes when he devotes his effort to demonstrating the superiority of his own powers of interpretation at the expense of the poet's. Protagoras promotes himself as the more qualified moral authority worthy of the endorsement that tradition gives poets. Socrates sets out to challenge Protagoras, but not, of course, on behalf of the poets. Socrates disputes the sophist's reasoning and challenges a primary presupposition that Protagoras shares with the poets. As we saw in our discussion of the *Apology*, Socrates aims to subvert the poets' reputation for wisdom by emphasizing that they lack knowledge of their poetry's meaning. The traditional education that Protagoras alludes to here relies on the poet's reputation as a source of wisdom and moral instruction. Protagoras would appropriate the poet's authority as his own by advancing objections to the poet's grasp of his verses' meaning. These objections effectively commend his own understanding as superior to the poets' knowledge of their own poetry. Although Protagoras and Socrates concur in disputing the poets' authority over the significance of their verse, their reasons differ as radically as sophistical aims differ from Socratic ones.

The Simonides episode divides into two parts. In the first Socrates and Protagoras spar over Protagoras's criticisms of the poem (339b–342a). In the second Socrates cuts short the dialectical exchange and presents his own comprehensive reading of the poem (342a–348a). Throughout the episode, Socrates' tone is humorous, yet unmistakably agonistic. With Protagoras's comparative humorlessness, Plato conveys a pointed contrast between the sophist's vulnerability and the humor and control that mark Socrates' mastery and detachment. This contrast is apparent from their initial exchange, following Protagoras's opening charge that Simonides is inconsistent. According to Protagoras, Simonides' poem both affirms that it is difficult for a man to become truly good and denies it by rejecting Pittacus's maxim that "it is hard to be good." After setting out his criticism, Protagoras accepts a "noisy round of applause" from his audience with which Socrates signals his agreement by describing Protagoras's effect on him as being "hit by a good boxer" (339d10). Socrates will adopt this athletic simile again in his description of Simonides' purpose.[5] Socrates then requests Prodicus's help, while he confesses in an aside to be stalling for time. If Socrates claims in earnest that Protagoras has left him helpless, it is not borne out by his actions. He enlists Prodicus merely to agree with his sound proposal that the apparent contradiction is resolved if we are careful to distinguish "being" from "becoming." In that case what Simonides says is perfectly consistent: it is not hard (but in fact impossible) to *be* good, but it is difficult to *become* good. Socrates appears to throw sus-

[5] 343c2–6: "Then Simonides, ambitious for philosophical fame, saw that if he could score a takedown against this saying, as if it were a famous wrestler, and get the better of it, he would himself become famous in his own lifetime."

picion on his own retort by claiming that it is an example of Prodicus's "special art" (340b1). But in fact he invokes a legitimate distinction.[6] Socrates has answered Protagoras's challenge with ease.

Protagoras loses no time, however, in renewing his attack from a new angle. Simonides can be accused of monumental ignorance if he claims that it is not difficult to be good, "if he says the possession of virtue is so trivial when everyone agrees it is the hardest thing in the world" (340e5–7). Socrates' reply is especially contrived, as it mocks Protagoras by soaring over his head. The joke Socrates and Prodicus play on Protagoras apes a sophistic reply that Protagoras takes at face value. In mock defense of Simonides, they propose that by "hard" the poet really meant "bad," and that the offense for which he criticized Pittacus was a misuse of terms. They attribute to Simonides a sophistic mindset that is specifically Prodicean, and portray the poet as a sophist given to elaborating hair-splitting points about terminology. Protagoras falls for the bait when, in his fully unsuspecting reply, he disputes that Simonides could have meant "bad" by "hard." When Socrates confesses that he and Prodicus were merely testing Protagoras to see if he could defend himself, Protagoras has been made to seem the fool.

It may appear that Socrates lets Protagoras's criticism stand when Socrates concludes this exchange by *agreeing* that "hard" cannot possibly mean "bad" in the poem since in that case Simonides would be saying that it is bad to be good. Simonides cannot possibly mean that it is bad to be good, Socrates reasons, since later in the ode he says that God alone has the privilege of being good. The observant reader, however, will see that with these remarks Socrates indirectly, but devastatingly, refutes Protagoras's criticism. The line Socrates quotes, "God alone can have this privilege," is said to be the phrase following the excerpt Protagoras quoted earlier:

Nor is Pittacus' proverb in tune
however wise a man he was.
Hard it is to be good, he said.

(339c3–5)

By quoting the next line Socrates shows that Simonides meant to say that it is *impossible* for a human being to be good. The result restores the con-

---

[6] Simonides could not have intended to make the *Platonic* distinction between γενέσθαι and ἔμμεναι (see U. v. Wilamowitz-Moellendorff, *Sappho und Alkaios* (Berlin, 1913), p. 167), but could nevertheless have recognized a less loaded distinction between the two (see Woodbury 1953, p. 140; Parry 1965; Taylor 1976, pp. 143–44). For a different view see Frede 1986, pp. 739–40. Socrates does not suggest that the interpretation is implausible by crediting Prodicus with the distinction. As we have seen, he misleads Protagoras into thinking that he is merely splitting hairs as the sophist might, when he is actually introducing a legitimate distinction.

text that Protagoras's quotation had obscured. Protagoras had taken a line out of context and thereby distorted the meaning of the poem. Socrates has resolved the apparent inconsistency with which Protagoras has charged Simonides,[7] and has successfully defended Simonides against the sophist's complaint that the poet is ignorant. Protagoras emerges exposed as a fool using dubious methods, and Socrates ends firmly established as master of the sophists' own game. Socrates' effort has not, however, been a mere "mock display of the sophistic art."[8] Socrates has ridiculed sophistic methods, to be sure, but while also successfully refuting Protagoras on matters of substance. He has used the pretense of indulging in mere satire to strike a damaging blow against his sophist opponent.

Socrates as Sophistic Interpreter

Socrates now takes his turn to lead the conversation by presenting his own extended interpretation of Simonides' poem. Socrates' interpretation is comprehensive in its attempts to understand the poem as a whole and so avoid the sophist's heavy-handed partiality. He offers an account of the poem's overall purpose and of how different sections contribute to that purpose. Socrates explicitly contrasts this approach with the one Protagoras took earlier:

> The poem is full of details that testify to its excellent composition; indeed, it is a lovely and exquisitely crafted piece, but it would take a long time to go through it from that point of view. Let's review instead the overall structure and intention of the ode . . . (344a7–b4)

Protagoras had suggested an approach to poetry that looks to those "details" that testify to whether a poem is well crafted or not (cf. 339a). It may appear that the contrast Socrates has in mind is one that contrasts style with substance, or form with content. But notice that Protagoras himself questions Socrates on matters of substance when he asks whether Simonides contradicts himself in saying both that it is hard to become good, and that Pittacus was wrong to say that it is hard to be good. So if Socrates intends to contrast Protagoras's approach with his own, the difference must be something other than the contrast between such matters of form and content. Socrates clarifies the sort of distinction he has in mind when he proposes to "review the overall structure and intention of the ode, which is from beginning to end a refutation of Pittacus' maxim" (344b3–5). Soc-

---

[7] Socrates' proposal of a distinction between being and becoming is in fact one of the most plausible way of resolving the apparent contradiction in the poem. For other possibilities and their disadvantages, see Taylor 1976, pp. 143–44.

[8] Frede 1986, p. 739.

rates will present a *unified* account of the entire poem, whereas the piece-meal method Protagoras illustrates takes an approach that permits discussing isolated matters of style or substance with no attempt to discern a contribution to any overall intention or meaning.

Socrates proposes, then, that the overall meaning and structure of the poem is to be discovered in Simonides' attempt to refute Pittacus's famous maxim, "It is hard to be good." Socrates' irony is unconcealed as he describes Pittacus's maxim as exhibiting Spartan philosophical wisdom and the philosophical style of laconic brevity that the Spartans revere as the sign of a truly educated man. He can hardly be speaking in earnest when he claims that the Spartans "have the best education in philosophy and debate" (342d5–6).[9] In any case, Socrates states his thesis that Simonides' poem aims systematically to refute Pittacus's maxim. The poet takes this as his aim, Socrates is careful to note, because of his ambition for philosophical fame. The agonistic subtext of the poem has as its aim winning, not truth, as Socrates' metaphors suggest: Simonides wants to "score a takedown" against Pittacus's saying, "as if it were a famous wrestler" (343c3–4). Simonides, we are told, is motivated to defeat Pittacus "so that he would himself become famous in his own lifetime" (343c5–6). There is no suggestion that Simonides defends his view because he thinks that it is correct. On the contrary, Socrates casts doubt on Simonides' philosophical honesty by citing his ambition and his desire for fame.

Socrates argues for his reading of the poem's first stanza with citations of grammatical points that would support the view that the poem's first line opposes Pittacus's maxim. According to Socrates, the presence of the antithetical particle *men* and the position of "truly" show that Simonides is addressing the Pittacus maxim as an opponent. Pittacus says it is hard to be good; Simonides rebuts this by saying, "No, but it is hard for a man to become good, Pittacus, truly" (343d4–7). Although Socrates' reading of the particle's significance is possible, if not entirely convincing, his treatment of the word "truly" appears to be deliberately strained.[10] Indeed, this focus on the fine points of grammar seems so out of character for Socrates, and so typical of sophistic methods, that it becomes unclear where the serious argument ends and the parody begins.

Socrates goes on to present the substance of his account by quoting and paraphrasing the poem and by supplying a line of thought to defend the views he finds there. His analysis of the second stanza concludes that the poem's first part maintains "that it is impossible to be a good man and continue to be good, but possible for one and the same person to become good and also bad, and those are best for the longest time whom the gods love"

---

[9] See Taylor 1976, p. 144.
[10] See Taylor 1976, p. 145.

(345c1–5). In his paraphrases and explanations, Socrates elicits from the stanza a distinctively Socratic view: that goodness consists in knowledge, and badness in ignorance (344e–345). According to Socrates, the third and fourth stanzas continue the attack against Pittacus. Again, Socrates takes great pains to read the poem as espousing views that are consistent with his own doctrine. It may appear that when Simonides says, "All who do no wrong willingly / I praise and love. / Necessity not even the gods resist," he admits the possibility of doing wrong willingly, which would contradict a central Socratic doctrine (345d). But Socrates reads the passage otherwise, taking "willingly" together with what follows rather than with what precedes it. On this reading, Simonides claims that he willingly praises and loves those who do no wrong. Socrates thus arrives at a reading that understands Simonides to address to Pittacus reflections on who is worthy and who is unworthy of praise and blame. Simonides is not a severely critical person, and willingly praises not only those who perform noble actions, but also those who merely refrain from wrongdoing. He would not have criticized Pittacus had his view been "even moderately reasonable and true" (346e8), but he does censure Pittacus because Pittacus has "lied blatantly yet with verisimilitude about extremely important issues" (347a2–3).

Socrates' interpretation is manifestly perverse when read in accordance with his avowed methodology. His focus on showing how Simonides' poem systematically serves its author's purposes relies on the assumption that to find the meaning of a poem is to discover and to demonstrate what the author's overall purpose is and how that purpose is carried out. At the conclusion of the interpretation Socrates reiterates that he has sought to give an account of "what I think was going through Simonides' mind when he composed this ode."[11] Socrates invokes this thoroughly intentionalist notion of literary interpretation as one that is familiar and well known to the sophists. The interpreter focuses on the poet and appeals to biographical features to help explain the poem's meaning. It is specifically when Socrates is understood to be giving an account of how the poem plays out Simonides' intentions that the interpretation slides into the extravagant and perverse. The unifying idea of Socrates' interpretation, that in the poem Simonides aims to refute Pittacus's maxim, stands as perfectly plausible. As we have seen, Socrates has already foreshadowed his interpretation by drawing the distinction between being and becoming. The sections of the poem Socrates quotes support well enough the idea that Simonides argues that it is impossible for a man to be truly (always) good. The third stanza says as much explicitly, that it is impossible to find a blameless man:

[11] ταῦτά μοι δοκεῖ, ὦ Πρόδικε καὶ Πρωταγόρα, ἦν δ᾽ ἐγώ, Σιμωνίδης διασούμενος πεποιηκέναι τοῦτο τὸ ᾆσμα (347a3–5).

Therefore never shall I seek for the impossible,
cast away my life's lot on empty hope, a quixotic quest
for a blameless man among those who reap
the broad earth's fruit,
but if I find him you will have my report.

(345c6–11)

Socrates' elaboration of Simonides' position, however, immediately invites suspicion. For example, at 345a–c Socrates imputes to the following lines the notion that "faring well" amounts to knowledge, and that "faring ill" is being ignorant:

Faring well, every man is good;
Bad, faring ill.

(344e7–8)

As an account of Simonides' intentions, this interpretation is indeed, as one commentator charges, "anachronistic and whimsical."[12] Its tendentious importation of a Socratic understanding of what it means to fare well or ill would have been unavailable to Simonides, who is more likely to have kept to a more conventional idea, such as that faring well and ill depend solely on the external forces of fortune mentioned at the beginning of the second stanza.[13]

Again, Socrates' reading of the third stanza seems forced and, as one commentator says, a "blatant perversion of the plain sense of the poem."[14] When Simonides says that "All who do no wrong willingly / I praise and love. / Necessity not even the gods resist" (345d3–5), he is likely to have in mind the conventional assumption that men sometimes cannot help doing wrong (leaving open the possibility that men *can* do wrong willingly). It is still less likely that he intended anything consistent with the thesis discussed later in the *Protagoras* that no one does wrong willingly (requiring the strained reading that takes "willingly" with what follows it rather than with what precedes).

However, it is not just that Socrates strains the plain sense of the poem and employs questionable arguments. He also adopts throughout his interpretation the anti-Socratic stance of a dogmatist seeking agreement between his own views and Simonides', rather than the position we have been taught to expect from him, of an inquirer pursuing knowledge in a text that owes its ultimate origins to the gods. Socrates apes the sophistic method of aiming solely to secure agreement in belief, rather than employing standards of inquiry to elucidate and establish whether or not a particular view

[12] Taylor 1976, pp. 145–46.
[13] "But that man inevitably is bad / whom incapacitating misfortune throws down." See Taylor's comparison with Theognis (Taylor 1976, p. 145).
[14] Taylor 1976, p. 146.

is reasonable. The particularly Socratic views that Socrates claims to discover in Simonides' poem are the provisional products of Socratic inquiry, subject to revision and modification. For the dialectical, and the comic purposes of this interpretation, however, Socrates allows himself to appear to hold them dogmatically and to aim solely to establish consonance between his own views and those of a traditionally respected poet. This is Socrates at his ironic best, imitating an approach that reverses the course of Socratic inquiry as the *Apology* sets it out.[15]

It is interesting in this regard to compare Xenophon's portrait, which, without Plato's irony and satirical intent, vulgarizes Socrates' engagement with poetry in a similar way. Xenophon defends Socrates against the charge that he cites the poets' authority to lend credence to immoral views. His accusers claim, for example, that Socrates cites Hesiod's line, "No work is a disgrace, but idleness is a disgrace" (*Works and Days* 309), to teach his companions to be tyrants and evildoers, reading the line as "an injunction to refrain from no work, dishonest or disgraceful, but to do anything for gain."[16] Xenophon defends Socrates by claiming that he interpreted the line differently, to mean that no *good* work is a disgrace, but immoral occupations are types of idleness and disgraceful. Xenophon undoubtedly has good intentions, but the emended view he presents could still, by Plato's lights, be said to portray Socrates negatively. Although Xenophon has Socrates extracting noble sentiments from poetry, he depicts him as behaving in a dogmatic and preacherly mode, sophistically seeking poetic authorities who agree with what appear to be dogmatically held tenets. This is a far cry from Socrates' program of antidogmatic inquiry in the *Apology*.

The Puzzle

When Socrates concludes his reading of the poem and says that his account has shown "what was going through Simonides' mind when he composed

[15] Pappas (1989) misses the irony when he suggests that Socrates' interpretation earnestly applies an excessive principle of charity. What Pappas calls Socrates' "search for truth" (p. 249) in the poem is precisely not an investigation into truth, but a sophistical search for *agreement* with views that he pretends to hold dogmatically. Contrast R. Scodel, "Literary Interpretation in Plato's *Protagoras*," *Ancient Philosophy* 6 (1986), pp. 34–35, who sees correctly that Socrates' seeking agreement is meant to demonstrate a faulty method of interpretation and point the way to a different, Socratic method for reading texts.

[16] *Memorabilia* 1. 2. 56 (cf. 57–61). According to Xenophon, Socrates' accusers also claim that he interpreted the description of Odysseus at *Iliad* 2. 188 as approval of chastising the common and the poor (Odysseus uses deference and tact to reprimand kings, but force when he is dealing with men of the people). Xenophon retorts that Socrates offered no such interpretation, but instead took the passage to illustrate that "those who render no service either by word or deed, who cannot help army or city or the people itself in time of need, ought to be stopped, even if they have riches in abundance, above all if they are insolent as well as inefficient" (1. 2. 59).

the poem," we have ample reason to view the interpretation as perverse and implausible, and therefore to look for an explanation for why Socrates invests effort in a bad interpretation of the poem. He appears to have done so not only to ridicule the sophists,[17] but also to illustrate the general skeptical claim he makes at the conclusion of his interpretation, that it is impossible to decide what a poet means:

> . . . when well-educated gentlemen drink together, you will not see girls playing the flute or the lyre or dancing, but a group that knows how to get together without these childish frivolities, conversing civilly no matter how heavily they are drinking. Ours is such a group, if indeed it consists of men such as most of us claim to be, and it should require no extraneous voices, not even of poets, who cannot be questioned on what they say. When a poet is brought up in discussion, almost everyone has a different opinion about what he means, and they wind up arguing about something they can never finally decide. The best people avoid such discussions and rely on their own powers of speech to entertain themselves and test each other. (347d3–348a2)

People will always have different opinions about what a poet means, and the oppositions between their contrary opinions can never finally be decided. The poet himself is unavailable to answer questions. Socrates' suggestion that the poet would be able to illuminate the meaning of his poetry must be taken ironically, given that the *Apology* showed that, even when he is available, the poet's gift cannot aid him in illuminating his own poetry or help him understand what his verses mean. Socrates explained this phenomenon by denying that the poet is equipped by his gift to contribute on any exegetical question of what his poem means or of what he himself means by it. Notice that when in the *Protagoras* Socrates says that "the best people avoid such discussions" he refers not generally to any discussions about the interpretation of poetry, but specifically to discussions about *poets* and what they mean. The conversations he advises his audience to avoid speculate about the poet's intentions.

If we take into account only the evidence we have so far discussed, we might be tempted to conclude that Socrates' interpretation of Simonides' poem carries out only the destructive aims of humiliating Protagoras and denouncing the sophists' literary-critical discussions. There are, however, some general indications that Socrates has a more constructive purpose as well. At the beginning of their conversation about Simonides' poem, Socrates offers an explicit indication that the interpretation of poetry is a task he takes seriously. When Protagoras asks Socrates if he should recite the poem, Socrates replies: "I told him there was no need, for I knew the

---

[17] Vlastos (1991) emphasizes Socrates' manifest cruelty in dealing with Protagoras, but tends to see the contest between the two men in quotidian terms of social one-upmanship.

poem, and it happened to be one to which I had given especially careful attention" (339b5–6). Some have been tempted to treat as purely ironic Socrates' claim to have already given careful attention to Simonides' poem. Ferrari, for example, presumes that Socrates' admission that he is stumped by Protagoras's questions (339c11–12), and his stalling for more time (339e3–4) belie his claim to have already examined the poem carefully. According to Ferrari, when Socrates claims to have carefully studied the poem, we are led to suspect that he has given careful attention only to what he takes the poem to be about: the difficulty of becoming good.[18] I would suggest, however, that Socrates' avowal that he has studied the poem should be taken at face value. As we have seen, his fumblings over the interchange with Protagoras and his stalling for time betray no unfamiliarity with the poem, but rather contribute to a rhetorical design aimed at ridiculing Protagoras. Socrates' ability to quote the poem from memory as well as the well-worked-out interpretation he goes on to present each attests to his prior study. His self-deprecations resonate with an indirect criticism of Protagoras and his sophistic methods: there is a suggestion that Socrates is taken off guard because Protagoras deals with the poem in a way that Socrates has not in the past deemed productive. This picture of a Socrates who takes poetry seriously is not uniquely Platonic. As we have seen, Xenophon shares it in his depiction of Socrates interpreting passages from the great poets.[19]

If we take the interpretation Socrates presents in the *Protagoras* to be the fruit of his previous study—and it is only natural to do so, given its polished presentation—we face the difficulties of discerning its *un*ironic significance, and of reconciling the remarks we have already considered briefly, which appear to undermine any attempt to credit Socrates with offering a sincere reading of the poem (347d3–e7). One scholar facing this problem has proposed the ingenious hypothesis that the concluding remarks undermining the value of literary criticism were originally meant to follow Socrates' initial discussion of the poem with Protagoras (339a–343). On this view, there was a "*Proto-Protagoras*" in which Socrates' extended interpretation of the poem (342a–347d) did not exist. For various reasons, Plato later interpolated Socrates' interpretation along with what appear to be references to the *Symposium* at 347d–e.[20] According to this hypothesis, discussion of the poem originally ended at 343c5, followed at 347eff. by Socrates' reasons for urging his audience to avoid the interpretation of poetry. Unfortunately, however, this proposal fails to solve the problem. Even if we were to accept the notion of a later interpolation, we would still be left with the question of why Plato later inserted a section that renders the whole inconsistent.

[18] Ferrari 1989, p. 101.
[19] *Memorabilia* 1. 2. 56–61.
[20] Frede 1986, pp. 746–50.

Socrates against the Sophists

We need an alternative that allows us to makes sense of Socrates' interpretation as serious as well as to retain the text as we have it. Commentators have suggested candidates for the "serious" purpose of Socrates' interpretation that include, for example, defending Simonides from Protagoras's attack and showing Protagoras that poetry is not the proper venue for the investigation of virtue, or clarifying the difference between sophistic and philosophic teaching.[21] But each of these suggestions links Socrates' purpose with the specific context of the *Protagoras,* and none is readily applicable to a context outside of the dialogue. By having Socrates allude to his previous careful study of the poem, Plato suggests that Socrates' interpretation has a serious purpose that reaches beyond the narrow scope of his discussion with Protagoras. Such a purpose, I would suggest, comes to light indirectly, from what is most blatantly *anti*-Socratic about this interpretation. As he often does in other contexts, Socrates here speaks past his immediate audience with a layer of tacit meaning.

The sophists listening to Socrates' interpretation fail to grasp that he is ridiculing the intentionalist presuppositions of their own methods of literary criticism and the relativism to which it inevitably leads. Plato draws our attention to this fact with Hippias's remark at the end of Socrates' speech: "I am favorably impressed by your analysis of this ode, Socrates. I have quite a nice talk on it myself, which I will present to you if you wish."[22] Hippias's remark may be taken to presume that he and Socrates share the relativist assumption that a poem is subject to more than one equally acceptable interpretation.[23] Here a sophist mistakes Socrates for a fellow sophist. What Hippias does not see—and what the reader is no doubt meant to grasp—is that, with his ludicrously anachronistic and tendentious interpretation, Socrates, far from maintaining sophistic presuppositions about the interpretation of poetry, has just attacked, by way of parody, analyses of poetry that focus on the author's intentions. Plato includes Hippias's remark to make it clear that Socrates' satire has gone over the heads of his audience, except perhaps for Alcibiades, whose abrupt dismissal of Hippias's suggestion alludes to the sophist's self-absorbed lack of comprehension.[24] Socrates' attack on sophistic methods of interpretation does not aim to convince the sophists themselves; that attempt, Plato suggests, would be futile, since the sophists' overwhelming sense of self-importance

---

[21] Ferrari 1989, pp. 102–3; Carson 1992, p. 128.

[22] 347a6–b2.

[23] As Demos 1999, p. 33, rightly points out.

[24] "Yes, Hippias . . . some other time, though. What should be done now is what Socrates and Protagoras agreed upon, which is for Socrates to answer any questions Protagoras may still have to ask, or if he so chooses, to answer Socrates' questions" (347b3–7).

prevents them even from recognizing that they are being ridiculed. The attack is directed, rather, at convincing Plato's readers. Unlike the sophists who witness Socrates' performance, the reader grasps that Socrates' dazzling, but fundamentally implausible, interpretation of Simonides' ode has indirectly launched a forceful attack on any view of literary criticism aimed at reconstructing the author's intentions. In his concluding remarks (347c–348a), Socrates makes explicit the connection between intentionalist interpretation and the sophistic relativism Hippias represents. According to Socrates, in discussions that attempt to reconstruct the author's intentions, "people wind up arguing about something they can never finally decide," since the poets "cannot be questioned on what they say."[25] Even here, Socrates maintains the persona of a sophist. He speaks as though he shares the assumption that an accurate interpretation of a poem would discover the poet's intentions. The interpretation that Socrates has just presented, however, distances him from that assumption by ridiculing, with its anything-goes approach, the relativism to which it inevitably leads. Moreover, we know from the Socratic theory of inspiration in the *Ion* and its complement in the *Apology* that, in Socrates' view, the poet *has* no intentions about his poem's meaning or at least none that his poetic gift supplies him. Socrates' concluding remarks in the *Protagoras*'s Simonides episode, then, should not be taken at face value, as they are standardly understood. Socrates continues to speak past his audience of sophists; he speaks as if he agrees with their assumptions in order to make his case for abandoning the current discussion of poetry. The audience of readers whom Socrates addresses can view critically the sophist's intentionalist assumptions that lead to relativism about poetry's interpretation.

If instead we did take Socrates' remarks in earnest and as his final word on the subject of poetry, then we might naturally be led to an interpretation of this episode similar to the one Ferrari offers. Ferrari understands Socrates' final remarks to state categorically that the enterprise of interpreting poetry is pointless. According to Ferrari, the *Protagoras* devotes this entire episode to promoting the thesis that confines poetry's function to the merely emblematic or inspirational. On his view, Socrates dramatizes his point with the *Protagoras*'s perverse reading of Simonides' poem that treats poetry in precisely the wrong way: by imputing to it philosophical views and arguments, rather than celebrating its theatrical and inspirational value.[26] As Ferrari reads Socrates' concluding remarks, they express his view by explicitly denying that poems have determinate meanings.

But we must look closely at Socrates' concluding remarks, because what he states is not quite the nihilist alternative to sophistic poetics that Ferrari

---

[25] 347e.
[26] Ferrari 1989, pp. 99–103.

and others have attributed to him. Socrates claims only that discussions can never reach agreement about the *poet's intentions*. The argument he offers for this claim—that the poet is not available to decide the issue—disguises the actual reason Socratic poetics gives for rejecting it: that the poet's inspiration is incompatible with his having any intentions at all about his poem's meaning. Socrates' claim about the futility of intentionalist interpretation, however, implies neither that poems lack determinate meaning, nor that inquiry must fail to discover what they mean. Provided that the meaning of a poem is identified with its poet's intentions, Socrates rightly tells Protagoras that investigation of questions of virtue should not proceed via the interpretation of poetry. But Socrates is discouraging only the interpretation of poetry as his sophist interlocutors understand it. According to Socrates' own poetics and freed of the sophists' assumptions, poetry's contribution to the investigation of virtue depends on its own divinely inspired and inquisitively discoverable meaning.

The *Protagoras* signals the relativist implication of the sophistical treatment of poetry with the person of Hippias, who evidently overlooks Socrates' effort at parody and finds nothing untoward in Socrates' example of egregiously bad interpretation. Hippias's remarks, we noted above, intimate that his view may allow even inconsistent interpretations of a given poem to share equal legitimacy. Still in his parodic role of unbridled sophist, Socrates intimates a skeptical argument for this relativism: Socrates' interpretation has demonstrated that by appealing to the text of the poem alone, one cannot uncover the author's intentions. To discover the author's intentions, one must look beyond the text and ask the author himself. So where the author himself is unavailable, one must draw the relativist conclusion that Hippias personifies. The way is thus left open for the sophistical position that interpretations can be evaluated only in terms of how persuasively they affect their audience. We have seen how Protagoras's interpretation attempts to capitalize on this relativism in his effort to appear more clever than Simonides. Protagoras does not attempt to give an account of the poem's meaning or of Simonides' intentions; he simply faults Simonides for inconsistency. Socratic poetics, as we know from the *Ion* and *Apology*, concurs with the *Protagoras*'s skepticism about attempts to discover the poet's intentions. For Socrates, however, this skepticism rests on the fact that the poet's inspiration ensures a lack of anything to know about the poet's intentions for his verse's meaning. Socratic poetics' alternative to the sophistic relativism is Socrates' view that their divine inspiration supplies poems with a morally significant meaning internal to them, and thus with something for an interpretation to be right or wrong about. Socrates' reading of Simonides' poem, then, when taken together with the *Ion* and *Apology*, is cautionary; his focus on Simonides' intentions adopts a counter-Socratic approach. In undercutting assumptions upon which typical literary interpretations proceed (including his own mock interpretation), Socrates indirectly reinforces his own view of how the interpretation of poetry can be valuable and advance the investigation of virtue. Of course, Protagoras's relativism prevents him from considering the possibility that poetry harbors truth or that inquiry could yield anything more than a personal opinion. Protagoras cannot grasp that the interpretation Socrates offers is anti-Socratic, but readers of the *Apology* and *Ion* can. In order to see how Socrates' reading of Simonides implies the outlines of a positive, Socratic reading, we need to turn to Socrates' interpretation of a text that shares many crucial features with poetry: the Delphic oracle's pronouncement that no man is wiser than Socrates. The principles and methods that Socrates brings to bear on this text in the *Apology* illustrate what I would suggest is the Socratic approach to the interpretation of poetry.

The Oracle, a Socratic Interpretation

The *Apology* illustrates successful Socratic interpretation with an example that applies Socratic inquiry to elicit the meaning of a divinely inspired text that is not a poet's verse, but Apollo's oracle that "no man is wiser than Socrates" (21a8). There is, of course, wide disagreement (to which I shall attempt to avoid contributing) about some of the main issues attached to Socrates' treatment of the oracle, such as the nature of Socratic ignorance.[27] Socrates introduces his autobiographical recounting of the oracle to explain what the wisdom is that he ascribes to himself as source of the popular Athenian prejudices against him:

> The fact is, men of Athens, that I have acquired this reputation on account of nothing else than a sort of wisdom. What kind of wisdom is this? Just that which is perhaps human wisdom. (20d6–8)

Socrates' reputation misrepresents this wisdom. Socrates has already traced the popular prejudices against him to misconceptions fixed in Aristophanes' comic portrait of him as a sophist in the *Clouds*.[28] In order to discover the correct account of the kind of wisdom he has, Socrates recounts the results of his friend Chaerophon's unbidden report from Delphi: the Pythia announced that no man is wiser than Socrates. Socrates responds with an expression of his peculiar ignorance: "for I am conscious that I am not at all wise" (21b4–5). This collision between the announcement from Delphi and his avowed ignorance presents Socrates with a riddle:

---

[27] See H. Benson, *Socratic Wisdom: The Model of Knowledge in Plato's Early Dialogues* (New York, 2000), for discussion and extensive bibliography.

[28] See *Apology* 19b–d.

What in the world does the god mean, and what riddle is he propounding? (21b3–4)

The fact that the oracle poses for Socrates a riddle and not merely a mundane generalization that contradicts something he knows makes it plain that Socrates takes the oracle to be divinely inspired. If, for example, Socrates had understood that his friend Crito had said that all Athenians are wise, he would have rejected that generalization as one that he knows is false on the ground that he is himself an exception. But Socrates does not reject the oracle as a generalization to which he knows he is an exception. Instead, he defers to the oracle as to a text backed by some superhuman source.[29] The result is a riddle: what is this wisdom that reconciles the oracle's generalization with Socrates' professed ignorance? Socrates' finding a riddle in the oracle, then, establishes that he takes the Pythia's saying to be divinely inspired, just as poetic verse is inspired.

The method Socrates applies to interpret the oracle and solve its riddle is, I would suggest, the same method Socratic poetics would employ to interpret poetry:

For a long time I was at a loss as to his meaning; then very reluctantly turned to some such investigation as this: I went to one of those reputed wise, thinking that there if anywhere I could refute the oracle and say to it: "This man is wiser than I, but you said I was." (21b7–c2)

The method Socrates chooses to apply to interpreting the oracle is dialogic inquiry aimed at discovering an interlocutor superior to himself in wisdom. This quest leads him to interview, among others, the poets. As I discussed earlier, the poets cannot provide counterexamples to the oracle's generalization because they lack the wisdom with which they are traditionally credited and which only the divine source of their inspiration can have. For other reasons, the politicians and craftsmen whom Socrates interviews also confirm the oracle's generalization.

The result of his inquisitive effort that included these interviews with the politicians, poets, and craftsmen is an insight that interprets the oracle by solving its riddle:

And it appears that he does not really say this of Socrates, but merely uses my name and makes me an example, as if he were to say: "This one of you, mortals, is wisest who, like Socrates, recognizes that he is in truth of no account in respect to wisdom." (23a7–b4)

Socrates arrives at this interpretation of the oracle by grasping a conception of wisdom new to him: the wisdom that the oracle attributes to Socra-

---

[29] Of course, Socrates' deference does not extend to his accepting the oracle's generalization at the expense of abandoning what he knows.

tes is none other than his ignorance. This solves the riddle by introducing
an idea of wisdom that reconciles Socrates' ignorance with the wisdom attributed to him in the oracle's generalization. The outcome supplies the
promised elucidation of the idea of wisdom that Socrates attributes to himself and to which he traces the popular misconceptions about him. The inquiry that produced an interpretation of the oracle both arrives at a new
conception of wisdom (and in this way offers an account of what the oracle means) and establishes that the oracle is true.

Socrates' success in interpreting the oracle emphasizes inquiry's role as
the Socratic method of interpretation. It also highlights the Delphic oracle's role as conveyer of divine wisdom to human audiences, the same role
that, according to Socratic poetics, the poet plays. To expect a poet's inspiration to aid his understanding of his own verses would be as out of place
as to consult the Pythia about the meaning of an oracle. A Socratic interpretation of a poem would, I suggest, by means of Socratic inquiry, provide an exposition of the poem's moral truths without resorting to any
speculation about the poet's intentions.[30] It may appear at first that Socratic inquiry and literary interpretation aim at different goals: inquiry evaluates the truth of some claim, whereas interpretation of a literary text tries
to say what the claim *is,* what the text *means.* Socrates' interpretation of
the oracle, however, provides a model of interpretation that combines these
two aims: Socrates both interprets the oracle's meaning *and* evaluates its
truth. A Socratic interpretation of poetry would follow this model by assuming that a poem has a meaning that expresses some truth, and then setting out to discover that meaning through Socratic inquiry.

By presenting a manifestly anti-Socratic interpretation, the *Protagoras*
intimates a Socratic interpretation of Simonides' ode that would follow the
model set out in the *Apology* by applying philosophical inquiry to extract
the poem's moral truths. In the interpretation he presents in the *Protagoras,* Socrates extracts from the poem doctrines that he defends elsewhere
in the dialogue, but the interpretation itself applies anti-Socratic methodology in failing to include such arguments, and instead simply maintaining
such doctrines dogmatically. A truly Socratic interpretation would include
an examination of the truth of the views attributed to the poem. We do not
necessarily need to look beyond the *Protagoras* itself for evidence that Plato
ultimately intends to contrast sophistic with Socratic methodology in the
Simonides episode; this contrast serves as a theme throughout the dialogue, for example in the ongoing tensions that surface regarding the con-

---

[30] We must thus qualify the claim that Socrates undermines the poetic text's authority
(Scodel 1986, p. 35). He could indeed be said to undermine its *dogmatic* authority, but he
maintains poetry's authority insofar as he holds that it harbors truth, at the same time he holds
that its truth is not immediately accessible and only available by applying to the poem methods of Socratic inquiry.

trast between the sophists' habit of extended speechmaking and the question and answer format of Socratic inquiry.[31] In the context of the *Protagoras* as a whole, the Simonides episode, I would suggest, functions to advance the dialogue's methodological theme by implicitly arguing against assumptions that ground sophistic interpretation and advocating instead the methods of Socratic inquiry.

Elsewhere, Socrates *explicitly* interprets Simonides Socratically. Book 1 of the *Republic* may be said even to set out the task of the entire dialogue as an attempt to arrive at the correct interpretation of Simonides' saying that it is just to give to each what is owed him (quoted by Polemarchus at 331e). When he and his interlocutors begin to attempt interpretation, Socrates exclaims that Simonides must be speaking in riddles just like a poet (332b). Socrates and the others take Simonides seriously; Socrates says that Simonides "is a wise and god-like man." But Socrates claims not to understand what he means (331e). Socrates remains more puzzled than Polemarchus about the meaning of the quotation because he anticipates how difficult it is to interpret. In the first book they do not arrive at a satisfactory interpretation. They refute the interpretation that takes it to mean that a just man should harm his enemies and benefit his friends, but they do not reject Simonides' text. Rather, they vow to reject any interpretation that interprets Simonides (and other wise men) in such a way that has him say something false (335e). When much later in the dialogue they define justice more satisfactorily, as a kind of harmony of the soul and analogously of the parts of the state, they finally do arrive at a satisfactory interpretation of Simonides. Socrates does not remind us of this, but harmony of the parts of the soul and the analogous parts of the state are interpretations of "giving to each what is owed him." The argument of the *Republic* can in this way be seen as an interpretation of Simonides' cryptic definition of justice; Socrates treats it in the same way he treats the oracle, as cryptically expressing a divine truth. His method of interpretation has been nothing less than the philosophical inquiry that constitutes the *Republic*'s discussion and definition of justice. The results of Socrates' interpretation are not ones that turn out to agree with a view he already held beforehand, but are new truths generated by the interpretation itself.

We have seen that Socrates fully accepts the poet's claim to divine inspiration, qualifies his endorsement of poetry's traditional role as fount of wisdom and exemplary morality, and wholly subverts the poets' various efforts to govern or suppress interpretation. These results depend primarily on Socrates' including poetry within the subject matter of Socratic inquiry. The distinction Socrates imposes between privileged poetic inspiration and

[31] See, for example, 329a–b.

the capacity for understanding poetry's significance undermines the poets' opposition to interpretation and locates the resources for interpreting poetry in all who engage in Socratic inquiry. It follows that Socrates' opposition to the poets' theories of poetry also opens to Socratic scrutiny the moral concepts, precepts, and exemplars that Athenian tradition trusted poetry to harbor. As Socratic poetics includes the interpretation of poetry within the examined life, it separates the poets' claim that poetry issues from a divine source from the Homeric inference that poetry therefore conveys divine knowledge to its audience. According to Socrates, what audiences earn when they interpret divinely inspired poetry is not any share of divine knowledge, but rather improved human wisdom. Like the Delphic oracle's pronouncement, poetry can have a divine source, but the wisdom that its Socratic interpretation can advance must be human wisdom.

Bibliographic References

Adam, J., and A. M. Adam. 1928. *Platonis Protagoras*. Cambridge.

Alden, M. J. "The Resonances of the Song of Ares and Aphrodite." *Mnemosyne* 50: 513–29.

Annas, J. 1999. *Platonic Ethics Old and New*. Ithaca and London.

Arthur, M. 1983. "The Dream of a World Without Women: Poetics and the Circles of Order in the *Theogony* Prooemium." *Arethusa* 16: 97–135.

Auerbach, E. 1953. "The Scar of Odysseus." In his *Mimesis: The Representation of Reality in Western Literature*. Trans. W. R. Trask. Princeton.

Austin, N. 1994. *Helen of Troy and Her Shameless Phantom*. Ithaca.

Babut, D. 1975. "Simonide moraliste." *Rev. Etud. Grecq.* 88: 20–62.

Barthes, R. 1977. "The Death of the Author." In *Image-Music-Text*. Essays Selected and Translated by S. Heath. New York.

Benson, H. 2000. *Socratic Wisdom: The Model of Knowledge in Plato's Early Dialogues*. New York.

Bergren, A. 1983. "Odyssean Temporality: Many (Re)Turns." In Rubino, C., and C. Shelmerdine, *Approaches to Homer*. Austin.

Blanchot, M. 1982. *The Sirens' Song*. Bloomington.

Bloom, H. 1994. *The Western Canon*. New York.

Booth, W. 1961. *The Rhetoric of Fiction*. Chicago.

Bowie, E. L. 1993. "Lies, Fiction and Slander in Early Greek Poetry." In C. Gill and T. P. Wiseman, eds., *Lies and Fiction in the Ancient World*. Austin.

Bowra, C. M. 1964. *Pindar*. Oxford.

Brandwood, L. 1992. "Stylometry and Chronology." In *The Cambridge Companion to Plato,* ed. R. Kraut. Cambridge.

Brooks, P. 1993. *Body Work: Objects of Desire in Modern Narrative*. Cambridge.

Brown, N. O., trans. 1953. *Theogony/Hesiod*. Indianapolis.

Bundy, E. L. 1962. *Studia Pindarica*. 2 pts. *University of California Studies in Classical Philology* 18.

Burnyeat, M. 1999. "Culture and Society in Plato's *Republic*." In *The Tanner Lectures on Human Values* 20. Salt Lake City.

Carson, A. 1992. "How Not to Read a Poem: Unmixing Simonides From *Protagoras*." *CP* 87: 110–30.

Clay, J. S. 1983. *The Wrath of Athena*. Princeton.

———. 1988. "What the Muses Sang: *Theogony* 1–115." *Greek, Roman and Byzantine Studies* 29: 323–33.

Cole, A. T. 1983. "Archaic Truth." *QUCC*, n.s. 13: 7–28.

Crotty, K. 1994. *The Poetics of Supplication*. Ithaca.

Curtius, E. R. 1953. *European Literature and the Latin Middle Ages*. Princeton.

Demos, M. 1999. *Lyric Quotation in Plato*. New York.

De Jong, I. J. F. 1985. "Eurykleia and Odysseus' Scar: *Odyssey* 19.393–466." *CQ* 35: 517–18.

Denniston, J. D., and D. Page. 1957. *Aeschylus, Agamemnon*. Oxford.

De Rachewiltz, S. W. 1987. *De Sirenibus: An Inquiry into the Sirens from Homer to Shakespeare*. Dissertation, Harvard University.

Detienne, M. 1996. *The Masters of Truth in Archaic Greece*. New York (English translation of *Les Maîtres de vérité dans la Grèce archaique*. Paris, 1967.)

Dodds, E. R. 1951. *The Greeks and the Irrational*. Berkeley.

Doherty, L. E. 1995. "Sirens Muses, and Female Narrators in the *Odyssey*." In B. Cohen, ed., *The Distaff's Side: Representing the Female in Homer's Odyssey*. New York.

Donlan, W. 1969. "Simonides Fr. 4D and P. Oxy. 2432." *TAPA* 100: 71–95.

Dover, K. J. 1970. *Aristophanes Clouds*. Oxford.

Duchemin, J. 1955. *Pindare poète et prophète*. Paris.

Eliade, M. 1959. *The Sacred and the Profane*. Trans. W. R. Trask. San Diego.

Fascher, E. 1927. ΠΡΟΦΗΤΗΣ. Geissen.

Feeney, D. C. 1991. *The Gods in Epic: Poets and Critics of the Classical Tradition*. Oxford.

Ferrari, G. 1988. "Hesiod's Mimetic Muses and the Strategies of Deconstruction." In A. Benjamin, ed., *Post-Structuralist Classics*. London and New York.

————. 1989. "Plato and Poetry." In G. A. Kennedy, ed., *The Cambridge History of Literary Criticism Volume One: Classical Criticism*. Cambridge: 102–3.

Finkelberg, M. 1998. *The Birth of Literary Fiction in Ancient Greece*. Oxford.

Ford, A. 1992. *Homer: The Poetry of the Past*. Ithaca.

Foucault, M. 1986. "What is an Author?" In P. Rabinow, ed., *The Foucault Reader*. New York.

Frede, D. 1986. "The Impossibility of Perfection: Socrates' Criticism of Simonides' Poem in the *Protagoras*." *Review of Metaphysics* 39: 729–53.

Friedländer, P. 1964. *Plato: The Dialogues*. Vol. 2. New York.

Frontisi-Ducroux, F. 1986. *La cithare d'Achille*. Rome.

Gantz, T. 1993. *Early Greek Myth: A Guide to Literary and Artistic Sources*. Baltimore and London.

Gentili, B. 1983. "Poeta e musico in Grecia." In *Oralità, Scrittura, Spettacolo,* ed. M. Vegetti. Turin.

Gianotti, G. F. 1975. *Per una poetica pindarica*. Torino.

Gill, C., and T. P. Wiseman, eds. 1993. *Lies and Fiction in the Ancient World*. Austin.

Goldhill, S. 1991. *The Poet's Voice: Essays on Poetics and Greek Literature*. Cambridge.

Gresseth, G. K. 1970. "The Homeric Sirens." *TAPA* 101: 203–18.

Griffith, M. 1983. "Personality in Hesiod." *Classical Antiquity* 2: 37–65.

Gundert, H. 1952. "Die Simonides-Interpretation in Platons *Protagoras*." In *Hermeneia: Festschrift Otto Regenbogen*. Heidelberg: 71–93.

Hainsworth, B., ed. 1993. *The Iliad: A Commentary. Volume 3: Books 9–12*. Cambridge.

Hamilton, R. 1974. *Epinikion: General Form in the Odes of Pindar*. The Hague.

Harriott, R. 1969. *Poetry and Criticism Before Plato*. London.

Heath, M. 1985. "Hesiod's Didactic Poetry." *CQ* 35: 245–63.

Irwin, T. H. 1977. *Plato's Moral Theory*. Oxford.

Jaeger, W. 1947. *Paideia*. Vol. 1, Trans. G. Highet. Oxford.

Janaway, C. 1995. *Images of Excellence: Plato's Critique of the Arts*. Oxford.

Kahn, C. H. 1979. *The Art and Thought of Heraclitus: An Edition of the Fragments with Translation and Commentary*. Cambridge.

———. 1996. *Plato and the Socratic Dialogues: The Philosophical Use of a Literary Form*. Cambridge.

Kirby, J. "Rhetoric and Poetics in Hesiod." *Ramus* 21: 34–60.

Kirkwood, G. 1982. *Selections From Pindar*. Chico.

Köhnken, A. 1976a. "Die Narbe des Odysseus: Ein Beitrag zur homerisch-epischen Erzähltechnik." *Antike und Abendland* 22: 101–14.

———. 1976b. *Die Funktion des Mythos bei Pindar*. Berlin.

Koller, H. 1956. "Das kitharodische Prooimion." *Philologus* 100: 159–206.

———. 1965. "ΘΕΣΠΙΣ ΑΟΙΔΟΣ." *Glotta* 43: 277–85.

Kraus, W. 1955. "Die Auffassung des Dichterberufs im früen Griechentum." *WS* 68: 65–87.

Kraut, R., ed. 1992. *The Cambridge Companion to Plato*. Cambridge.

Lamarque, P. 1990. "The Death of the Author: An Analytical Autopsy." *British Journal of Aesthetics* 30: 319–31.

Lamb, W. R. M. 1924. *Plato: Protagoras*. New York.

Lanata, G. 1963. *Poetica preplatonica*. Florence.

Latte, K. 1946. "Hesiods Dichterweihe." *Antike und Abendland* 2: 152–63.

Lattimore, R., trans. 1951. *The Iliad of Homer*. Chicago.

———, trans. 1967. *The Odyssey of Homer*. New York.

Lefkowitz, M. L. 1991. *First-Person Fictions: Pindar's Poetic "I."* Oxford.

Lewis, C. S. 1961. *A Preface to Paradise Lost*. New York.

Lombardo, S. and K. Bell, trans. 1992. *Protagoras/Plato*. Indianapolis.

Long, A. A. 2000. "A Critical Notice of Julia Annas, *Platonic Ethics Old and New*." *Oxford Studies in Ancient Philosophy* 19: 339–357.

Luther, W. 1935. *Wahrheit und Lüge*. Leipzig.

Lynn-George, M. 1988. *Epos: Word, Narrative and the Iliad*. London.

Mackie, P. 1997. "Song and Storytelling: An Odyssean Perspective." *TAPA* 127: 77–95.

Macleod, C. 1983. "Homer on Poetry and the Poetry of Homer." In his *Collected Essays*. New York.

Maehler, H. 1963. *Die Auffassung des Dichterberufs im frühen Griechentum bis zur Zeit Pindars*. Göttingen.

Marg, W. 1956. "Das erste Lied des Demodokos." In his *Navicula Chiloniensis*. Leiden.

———. 1971. *Homer über die Dichtung*. Münster.

Martin, R. 1992. "Hesiod's Metanastic Poetics." *Ramus* 21: 11–33.

Misch, G. 1973. *A History of Autobiography in Antiquity*. Vol. 1. Reprint, Westport.

Most, G. W. 1999. "The Poetics of Early Greek Philosophy." In *The Cambridge Companion to Early Greek Philosophy*, ed. A. A. Long. Cambridge.

Murdoch, I. 1977. *The Fire and the Sun: Why Plato Banished the Artists*. Oxford.

Murnaghan, S. 1987. *Disguise and Recognition in the Odyssey*. Princeton.

Murray, P. 1981. "Poetic Inspiration in Early Greece." *JHS* 101: 87–100.

———. 1983. "Homer and the Bard." In *Aspects of the Epic*, ed. T. Winnifrith, P. Murray, and K. Gransden. London.

————, ed. 1996. *Plato on Poetry*. Cambridge.

Nagy, G. 1989. "Early Greek Views of Poets and Poetry." In *The Cambridge History of Literary Criticism. Vol. I: Classical Criticism*. Cambridge.

Nehamas, A. 1999a. "Plato on Imitation and Poetry in *Republic* X." In Nehamas 1999c.

————. 1999b. "Plato and the Mass Media." In Nehamas 1999c.

————. 1999c. *Virtues of Authenticity: Essays on Plato and Socrates*. Princeton.

Newton, R. M. 1987. "Odysseus and Hephaestus in the *Odyssey*." *CJ* 83: 12–20.

Nussbaum, M. 1980. "Aristophanes and Socrates on Learning Practical Wisdom." *Yale Classical Studies* 26: 43–97.

Olsen, S. D. 1995. *Blood and Iron: Stories and Storytelling in Homer's Odyssey*. Leiden.

Page, D. L. 1962. *Poetae Melici Graeci*. Oxford.

Pappas, N. 1989a. "Socrates' Charitable Treatment of Poetry." *Philosophy and Literature* 13: 248–61.

————. 1989b. "Plato's Ion: The Problem of the Author." *Philosophy* 64: 381–89.

Parke, H. W. 1940. "A Note on the Delphic Priesthood." *CQ* 34: 85–89.

Parry, H. 1965. "An Interpretation of Simonides 4 (Diehl)." *TAPA* 96: 279–320.

Penner, T. 1992. "Socrates and the Early Dialogues." In Kraut 1992.

Pratt, L. H. 1993. *Lying and Poetry from Homer to Pindar: Falsehood and Deception in Archaic Greek Poetics*. Ann Arbor.

Pucci, P. 1977. *Hesiod and the Language of Poetry*. Baltimore.

————. 1979. "The Song of the Sirens." *Arethusa* 12: 121–32. (Reprinted in S. Schein, ed., *Reading the Odyssey*. Princeton, 1996.)

————. 1987. *Odysseus Polutropos: Intertextual Readings in the Odyssey and the Iliad*. Ithaca.

Puelma, M. 1989. "Der Dichter und die Wahrheit in der griechischen Poetik von Homer bis Aristoteles." *Museum Helveticum* 46: 121–32.

Quint, D. 1993. *Epic and Empire: Politics and Generic Form from Virgil to Milton*. Princeton.

Rabel, R. J. 1997. *Plot and Point of View in the Iliad*. Ann Arbor.

Race, W., ed. and trans. 1997. *Pindar*. 2 vol. Cambridge.

Redfield, J. M. 1973. "The Making of the *Odyssey*." In A. C. Yu, ed., *Parnassus Revisited*. Chicago.

————. 1975. *Nature and Culture in the Iliad*. Chicago.

Richardson, N. J. 1985. "Pindar and Later Literary Criticism in Antiquity." *Papers of the Liverpool Latin Seminar* 5: 383–401.

Rose, G. 1969a. "The Unfriendly Phaeacians." *TAPA* 100: 387–406.

————. 1969b. *The Song of Ares and Aphrodite*. Ph.D. dissertation, Berkeley.

Rösler, W. 1980. "Die Entdeckung der Fiktionalität." *Poetica* 12: 283–319.

Russell, D. A. 1981. *Criticism in Antiquity*. Berkeley.

Schadewalt, W. 1965. *Von Homers Welt und Werk*. Stuttgart.

Scodel, R. 1986. "Literary Interpretation in Plato's *Protagoras*." *Ancient Philosophy* 6: 25–37.

Scott, D. 1999. "Platonic Pessimism and Moral Education." *Oxford Studies in Ancient Philosophy* 17: 15–36.

Scully, S. 1981. "The Bard as Custodian of Homeric Society." *QUCC* 37: 67–83.

Segal, C. 1986. *Pindar's Mythmaking: The Fourth Pythian Ode.* Princeton.

———. 1988. "Kleos and its Ironies in the Odyssey." In H. Bloom, ed., *Homer's Odyssey.* New York.

———. 1992. "Bard and Audience in Homer." In *Homer's Ancient Readers,* ed. R. Lamberton and J. J. Keaney. Princeton.

———. 1994. *Singers, Heroes and Gods in the Odyssey.* Ithaca.

Setti, A. 1958. "La memoria e il canto: Saggio di poetica arcaica greca." *SIFC* 30: 129–71.

Sikes, E. E. 1931. *The Greek View of Poetry.* London.

Slatkin, L. 1991. *The Power of Thetis.* Berkeley.

Snell, B. 1982. *The Discovery of the Mind in Greek Philosophy and Literature.* Trans. T. G. Rosenmeyer. New York.

Sontag, S. 1961. "Against Interpretation." In her *Against Interpretation and Other Essays.* New York.

Sperdutti, A. 1950. "The Divine Nature of Poetry in Antiquity." *TAPA* 81: 209–40.

Stewart, D. 1976. *The Disguised Guest: Rank, Role, and Identity in the Odyssey.* Lewisburg.

Svenbro, J. 1976. *La Parole et le Marbre.* Lund.

Taylor, C. C. W. 1976. *Plato, Protagoras.* Oxford.

Thalmann, W. G. 1984. *Conventions of Form and Thought in Early Greek Poetry.* Baltimore.

Thornton, A. 1984. *Homer's Iliad: Its Composition and the Motif of Supplication.* Göttingen.

Tigerstedt, E. N. 1969. *Plato's Idea of Poetical Inspiration.* Helsinki.

———. 1970. "*Furor Poeticus:* Poetic Inspiration in Greek Literature before Democritus and Plato." *Journal of the History of Ideas* 31: 163–78.

Treu, M. 1965. "Von der Weisheit der Dichter." *Gymnasium* 72: 434–49.

Verdam, H. D. 1928. "De carmine Simonideo quod interpretatur Plato in Protagoro dialogo." *Mnemosyne* 56: 304–17.

Verdenius, W. J. 1972. "Notes on the Proem of Hesiod's *Theogony.*" *Mnemosyne* 25: 225–69.

———. 1987. *Commentaries on Pindar.* Vol. 1. *Mnemosyne* suppl. 97: 103–6.

Vernant, J.-P. 1965a. *Myth et pensée chez les Grecs.* Paris.

———. 1965b. "Aspects mythique de la mémoire et du temps." In Vernant 1965a.

Vivante, P. 1970. *Homeric Imagination: A Study of Homer's Poetic Perception of Reality.* Bloomington and London.

Vlastos, G. 1991. *Socrates: Ironist and Moral Philosopher.* Ithaca.

———. 1994. "The Socratic Elenchus: Method Is All." In his *Socratic Studies.* Cambridge.

Walsh, G. 1984. *The Varieties of Enchantment: Early Greek Views of the Nature and Function of Poetry.* Chapel Hill.

Webster, T. B. L. 1939. "Greek Theories of Art and Literature Down to 400 B.C.," *CQ* 33: 166–79.

West, M. L., ed. 1966. *Hesiod: Theogony.* Oxford.

Wilamowitz-Moellendorff, U. v. 1913. *Sappho und Alkaios.* Berlin.

Woodbury, L. 1953. "Simonides on Arete." *TAPA* 84: 135–63.

Woodruff, P., trans. 1983. *Plato, Two Comic Dialogues: Ion and Hippias Major.* Indiana.

Worman, N. 1997. "The Body as Argument: Helen in Four Greek Texts." *Classical Antiquity* 16: 151–203.

Young, D. C. 1983. "Pindar, Aristotle, and Homer: A Study in Ancient Criticism." *Classical Antiquity* 2: 156–70.

Index

Achilles: in Pindar, 67; as poet-figure, 11–12, 18–19
aesthetic theory, eroticism in, 3
aesthetic value, in Socratic poetics, 89–90, 94
Ajax, 71
Alcinoos, 35
allegorical tradition, 5, 78
allegories: of audience, 27–38; of inspiration, 88–95; of Muses, 27–34; of poet 27–34; of poetic performance and reception, 27–34
ambiguity: in Hesiodic poetics 44, 46, 52, 58; in Homeric poetics, 17, 19, 21–23, 25; in Pindaric poetics, 63, 66
antidogmatism: in *Apology,* 108; in Socratic poetics, 116
antitraditionalism, in Socratic poetics, 5–6, 74, 94
anxiety: in Hesiodic poetics, 50–51; in Pindaric poetics, 75–76
Aphrodite, 38
Apollo, 114
Apology (Plato), 4–5, 78–79, 81–83, 88, 90, 92–93, 97n, 98–102, 108–9, 112–16
appropriateness: in Pindaric poetics, 69–70; in Socratic poetics, 96
Ares, 38
Aristophanes, 4, 4n, 93, 114
Aristotle, *Poetics,* 12
Arthur, M., 45
athletic similes, 102, 105
audience: in Hesiodic poetics, 48–51, 53; in Homeric poetics, 14–15, 26–38; in Pindaric poetics, 74–76; as privy to divine knowledge, 26–7
Auerbach, E., 9–11, 34, 37–38
author: as character, 57–58; death of, 6; in Socratic poetics, 113
authority: in allegorical tradition, 78; in Hesiodic poetics, 44, 53, 56, 59, 61, 95, 98; in Homeric poetics, 17–18, 25–26, 32, 34, 39, 59, 61, 83, 95, 98; in Pindaric poetics, 61–62, 64, 66, 74, 77, 95,

98; in *Protagoras,* 101–2; in Socratic poetics, 4–6, 78, 82, 95, 98–99, 102, 116
autobiography, 55–59, 114

Barthes, R., 6
belief: in Plato, 92; in Socratic poetics, 91–92
Bloom, H., 10
Bowie, E. L., 20n
Brooks, Peter, 29

Calypso, 29, 31n
Charis (grace), 72, 75n
Cicero, 28n
Circe, 29; as poet-figure, 30–31
Clouds (Aristophanes), 4, 4n, 114
creativity, 13n, 62n, 90

danger: in Hesiodic poetics, 46; in Homeric poetics, 27–31
deception: in Hesiodic poetics, 32, 43–46, 51, 59, 72–73; in Homeric poetics, 27, 31–33; in Pindaric poetics, 68–73
De Jong, I. J. F., 10n
Delphic oracle, 63, 78, 92–93, 99, 114–18
Demodocus, 15–16, 18, 34–35, 38, 41, 96
Derrida, J., 45
desire: in Homeric poetics, 28–30; in Plato's view of poetry, 92
Detienne, M., 16n, 22, 24
didacticism, 41n, 51, 95
divinity: in Hesiodic poetics, 41–42, 47–54, 59, 75, 91; in Homeric poetics, 12, 14, 17–19, 23–24, 34, 39, 91; in Pindaric poetics, 64, 66–68, 91; in Socratic poetics, 6, 79, 81, 90, 94, 114–18
Dodds, E. R., 62–63
dogmatism: in *Euthyphro,* 82; in Pindar, 61, 74, 77; in *Protagoras,* 107–8

emotion: in Plato, 92; in Socratic poetics, 81, 91–92
eroticism: in aesthetic theory, 3, in Homeric poetics, 3, 28–34